teacher's friend

friend

publications

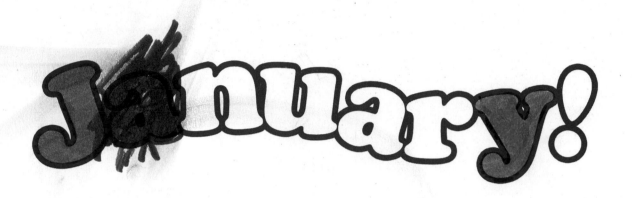

January!

a creative idea book
for the
elementary teacher

written and illustrated
by
Karen Sevaly

Copyright © Teacher's Friend,
a Scholastic Company
All rights reserved.
Printed in the U.S.A.

ISBN-13 978-0-439-50370-9
ISBN-10 0-439-50370-1

This book is dedicated
to teachers and children
everywhere.

Table of Contents

Making the most of it!

WHAT IS IN THIS BOOK:

You will find the following in each monthly idea book from Teacher's Friend Publications:

1. A calendar listing every day of the month with a classroom idea and mention of special holidays and events.

2. At least four student awards to be sent home to parents.

3. Three or more bookmarks that can be used in your school library or given to students by you as "Super Student Awards."

4. Numerous bulletin board ideas and patterns pertaining to the particular month and seasonal activity.

5. Easy-to-make craft ideas related to the monthly holidays and special days.

6. Dozens of activities emphasizing not only the obvious holidays, but also the often forgotten celebrations such as Chinese New Year and Martin Luther King Day.

7. Creative writing pages, crossword puzzles, word finds, booklet covers, games, paper bag puppets, literature lists and much more!

8. Scores of classroom management techniques and methods proven to motivate your students to improve behavior and classroom work.

HOW TO USE THIS BOOK:

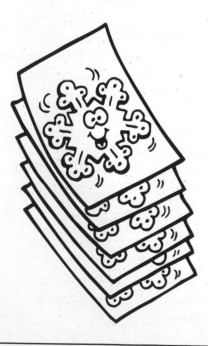

Every page of this book may be duplicated for individual class-room use.

Some pages are meant to be copied or used as duplicating masters. Other pages may be transferred onto construction paper or used as they are.

If you have access to a print shop, you will find that many pages work well when printed on index paper. This type of paper takes crayons and felt markers well and is sturdy enough to last. (Bookmarks work particularly well on index paper.)

Lastly, some pages are meant to be enlarged with an overhead or opaque projector. When we say enlarge, we mean it! Think BIG! Three, four or even five feet is great! Try using colored butcher paper or poster board so you don't spend all your time coloring.

ADDING THE COLOR:

Putting the color to finished items can be a real bother to teachers in a rush. Try these ideas:

1. On small areas, watercolor markers work great. If your area is rather large, switch to crayons or even colored chalk or pastels.

   (Don't worry, lamination or a spray fixative will keep color on the work and off of you. No laminator or fixative? That's okay, a little hair spray will do the trick.)

2. The quickest method of coloring large items is to start with colored paper. (Poster board, butcher paper or large construction paper work well.) Add a few dashes of a contrasting colored marker or crayon and you will have it made.

3. Try cutting character eyes, teeth, etc. from white typing paper and gluing them in place. These features will really stand out and make your bulletin boards come alive.

   For special effects, add real buttons or lace. Metallic paper looks great on stars and belt buckles, too.

LAMINATION:

If you have access to a roll laminator, then you already know how fortunate you are. They are priceless when it comes to saving time and money. Try these ideas:

1. You can laminate more than just classroom posters and construction paper. Try various kinds of fabric, wallpaper and gift wrapping. You'll be surprised at the great combinations you come up with.

   Laminated classified ads can be used to cut headings for current events bulletin boards. Colorful gingham fabric makes terrific cut letters or bulletin board trim. You might even try burlap! Bright foil gift wrapping paper will add a festive feeling to any bulletin board.

   (You can even make professional looking bookmarks with laminated fabric or burlap. They are great holiday gift ideas for Mom or Dad!)

2. Felt markers and laminated paper or fabric can work as a team. Just make sure the markers you use are permanent and not water-based. Oops, make a mistake! That's okay. Put a little ditto fluid on a tissue, rub across the mark and presto, it's gone! Also, dry transfer markers work great on lamination and can easily be wiped off.

LAMINATION:
(continued)

3. Laminating cut-out characters can be tricky. If you have enlarged an illustration onto poster board, simply laminate first and then cut it out with scissors or an art knife. (Just make sure the laminator is hot enough to create a good seal.)

One problem may arise when you paste an illustration onto poster board and laminate the finished product. If your paste-up is not 100% complete, your illustration and posterboard may separate after laminating. To avoid this problem, paste your illustration onto poster board that measures slightly larger than the illustration. This way, the lamination will help hold down your paste-up.

4. When pasting up your illustration, always try to use either rubber cement, artist's spray adhesive or a glue stick. White glue, tape or paste does not laminate well because it can often be seen under your artwork.

5. Have you ever laminated student-made place mats, crayon shavings, tissue paper collages, or dried flowers? You'll be amazed at the variety of creative things that can be laminated and used in the classroom or as take-home gifts.

PHOTOCOPIES AND DITTO MASTERS:

Many of the pages in this book can be copied for use in the classroom. Try some of these ideas for best results:

1. If the print from the back side of your original comes through the front when making a photocopy or ditto master, slip a sheet of black construction paper behind the sheet. This will mask the unwanted shadows and create a much better copy.

2. Several potential masters in this book contain instructions for the teacher. Simply cover the type with correction fluid or a small slip of paper before duplicating.

3. When using a new ditto master, turn down the pressure on the duplicating machine. As the copies become light, increase the pressure. This will get longer wear out of both the master and the machine.

4. Trying to squeeze one more run out of that worn ditto master can be frustrating. Try lightly spraying the inked side of the master with hair spray. For some reason, this helps the master put out those few extra copies.

MONTHLY ORGANIZERS:

Staying organized month after month, year after year can be a real challenge. Try this simple idea:

After using the loose pages from this book, file them in their own file folder labeled with the month's name. This will also provide a place to save pages from other reproducible books along with craft ideas, recipes and articles you find in magazines and periodicals. (*Essential Pocket Folders* by Teacher's Friend provide a perfect way to store your monthly ideas and reproducibles. Each *Monthly Essential Pocket Folder* comes with a sixteen-page booklet of essential patterns and organizational ideas. There are even special folders for *Back to School*, *The Substitute Teacher* and *Parent-Teacher Conferences*.)

You might also like to dedicate a file box for every month of the school year. A covered box will provide room to store large patterns, sample art projects, certificates and awards, monthly stickers, monthly idea books and much more.

BULLETIN BOARD IDEAS:

Creating clever bulletin boards for your classroom need not take fantastic amounts of time and money. With a little preparation and know-how, you can have different boards each month with very little effort. Try some of these ideas:

1. Background paper should be put up only once a year. Choose colors that can go with many themes and holidays. The black butcher paper background you used as a spooky display in October will have a special dramatic effect in April with student-made, paper-cut butterflies.

2. Butcher paper is not the only thing that can be used to cover the back of your board. You might also try fabric from a colorful bed sheet or gingham material. Just fold it up at the end of the year to reuse again. Wallpaper is another great background cover. Discontinued rolls can be purchased for a small amount at discount hardware stores. Most can be wiped clean and will not fade like construction paper. (Do not glue wallpaper directly to the board; just staple or pin in place.)

3. Store your bulletin board pieces in large, flat envelopes made from two large sheets of tagboard or cardboard. Simply staple three sides together and slip the pieces inside. (Small pieces can be stored in zip-lock, plastic bags.) Label your large envelopes with the name of the bulletin board and the month and year you displayed it. Take a picture of each bulletin board display. Staple the picture to your storage envelope. Next year when you want to create the same display, you will know right where everything goes. Kids can even follow your directions when you give them a picture to look at.

LETTERING AND HEADINGS:

Not every school has a letter machine that produces perfect 4" letters. The rest of us will just have to use the old stencil-and-scissor method. But wait, there is an easier way!

1. Don't cut individual letters as they are difficult to pin up straight, anyway. Instead, hand print bulletin board titles and headings onto strips of colored paper. When it is time for the board to come down, simply roll it up to use again next year. If you buy your own pre-cut lettering, save yourself some time and hassle by pasting the desired statements onto long strips of colored paper. Laminate if possible. These can be rolled up and stored the same way!

   Use your imagination! Try cloud shapes and cartoon bubbles. They will all look great.

2. Hand lettering is not that difficult, even if your printing is not up to penmanship standards. Print block letters with a felt marker. Draw big dots at the end of each letter. This will hide any mistakes and add a charming touch to the overall effect.

   If you are still afraid to freehand it, try this nifty idea: Cut a strip of poster board about 28" X 6". Down the center of the strip, cut a window with an art knife measuring 20" X 2". There you have it: a perfect stencil for any lettering job. All you need to do is write capital letters with a felt marker within the window slot. Don't worry about uniformity. Just fill up the entire window height with your letters. Move your poster-board strip along as you go. The letters will always remain straight and even because the poster board window is straight.

3. If you must cut individual letters, use construction paper squares measuring 4 1/2" X 6". (Laminate first if you can.) Cut the capital letters as shown. No need to measure; irregular letters will look creative and not messy.

       TF0100 January Idea Book

Calendar

January!

JANUARY

1ˢᵀ Today is NEW YEAR'S DAY! (Celebrate by asking your students to write their own New Year's resolutions!

2ᴺᴰ BETSY ROSS, designer of the first American flag, was born on this day in 1752. (Ask students to find pictures of the various flags that have flown over our country.)

3ᴿᴰ ALASKA became the United States' 49th state on this day in 1959. (Have your students find ten interesting facts about Alaska and then locate the state on the classroom map.)

4ᵀᴴ LOUIS BRAILLE, inventor of the alphabet for the blind, was born on this day in 1809. (Locate the Braille alphabet in an encyclopedia and have each child write his or her name in Braille.)

5ᵀᴴ Today is GEORGE WASHINGTON CARVER DAY! This multi-talented man invented more than 300 different products. (Ask students to list some of his accomplishments.)

6ᵀᴴ JOAN OF ARC was born on this day in 1412. She was burned at the stake for her religious beliefs. (Ask students to find out more about this courageous woman and report their findings to the class.)

7ᵀᴴ Today marks the birthdate of MIGUEL HIDALGO, father of Mexican independence. (Ask students to find out how this man helped his countrymen defeat the Spaniards.)

8ᵀᴴ ELVIS PRESLEY was born on this day in 1935. (Just for fun, play a couple of his songs during class exercise time.)

9ᵀᴴ The first school of SEEING EYE DOGS was founded on this day in 1929. (Ask students to list the many reasons a blind person might appreciate having a seeing eye dog.)

10ᵀᴴ OIL was discovered in Texas on this day in 1901. (Ask students why this valuable resource is called "Black Gold.")

11ᵀᴴ CIGARETTES were declared hazardous to our health on this day in 1964. (Have students list the various reasons people should not smoke.)

12TH   CHARLES PERRAULT, French writer and poet, was born on this day in 1628. Perrault wrote the famous tales of "Cinderella," "Puss and Boots" and "Little Red Riding Hood." (Read a version of one of these stories to your class, in his honor.)

13TH   STEPHEN FOSTER, composer of more than 175 songs, died on this day in 1826. (Join your class in a round of "Oh! Susanna" in commemoration.)

14TH   Missionary and humanitarian ALBERT SCHWEITZER was born on this day in 1875. (Ask students to find out what great things this man did and what prize he was awarded.)

15TH   MARTIN LUTHER KING, American civil rights leader, was born on this day in 1929. (Read Dr. King's "I have a dream" speech to your class. Ask them to write about their "dream" for America.)

16TH   Today is NATIONAL NOTHING DAY! (Ask children to invent their own holiday for this day. Have them choose colors, symbols and reasons for their holiday and present their ideas to the class.)

17TH   BENJAMIN FRANKLIN, American statesman and inventor, was born on this day in 1706. (Fly a kite with your class in celebration of Franklin's discovery of electricity.)

18TH   American heavyweight boxing champion MUHAMMAD ALI was born on this day in 1942. (Ali often recited short rhymes about himself such as "I run like a butterfly and sting like a bee!" Ask students to make up their own rhymes about themselves.)

19TH   ROBERT E. LEE, American Civil War general, was born on this day in 1807. (Ask students to list the states that fought on the side of the South during the Civil War.)

20TH   Today is PRESIDENTIAL INAUGURATION DAY in the United States. This event happens every four years when a new president takes the oath of office. (Watch this historical event on television with your class.)

21ST   MARY BRENT, the first woman in America to ask for the right to vote, was born on this day in 1648. (Ask your students to find out how many years it took for her request to be granted.)

22ND   Today is "ELSTEDENTOCHT" or the "Eleven Cities Race" in the Netherlands. Ice skaters race the 124 miles across the frozen canals of Holland. (Read Hans Brinker, by Mary Mapes Dodge, to your class in commemoration.)

23RD   JOHN HANCOCK, American patriot, was born on this day in 1737. (Ask students to locate a copy of the Declaration of Independence and then tell you why this man is so famous.)

24TH GOLD was discovered in SUTTER'S MILL, California, in 1848. (Can your students find Sutter's Mill, (Sacramento) on the classroom map?)

25TH The first WINTER OLYMPICS took place on this day in 1924 in Chamonix, France. (Ask students to list the various Winter Olympic events and write about the event in which they would like to compete.)

26TH DOUGLAS MACARTHUR, American WWII general, was born on this day in 1880. (Ask students to find out about his contribution and where he had promised to "return.")

27TH Austrian composer, WOLFGANG AMADEUS MOZART was born on this day in 1756. (Find a Mozart symphony and play it to your class during silent reading.)

28TH The United States COAST GUARD was established on this day in 1915. (Ask students why we need this branch of the armed services to protect our coast.)

29TH THOMAS PAINE, American political philosopher and writer, was born on this day in 1737. (Have students find the name of Paine's pamphlet that encouraged American independence.)

30TH The LIBRARY OF CONGRESS began operating on this day in 1815. Today, it houses more than 80 million books! (Ask your student to find out which president's collection of 6,000 books began it all.)

31ST HAM, a male chimpanzee, was rocketed into space during Project Mercury, in 1961. (Ask students how Ham helped the United States' space program.

DON'T FORGET THESE OTHER IMPORTANT HOLIDAYS:

CHINESE NEW YEAR (Between the middle of January and early March, the first day of the new moon using the Chinese calendar.)

January Calendar Symbols

January

Sunday	Monday	Tuesday	Wednesday	Thursday	Friday	Saturday

Winter Activities!

Winter Activities!

Warm up your students this winter with these inspiring activities. Even if you don't live in an area that has cold winters, you can still teach them about snowflakes, snow and icicles.

EXAMINING SNOWFLAKES

If you live in an area that receives snow each winter your students can study snowflakes. Even if you don't, students can still observe the icy patterns of winter frost or even the frost that accumulates inside a freezer.

Use a magnifying glass or a microscope to compare the patterns formed by the frost found in the freezer with frost found outdoors. Have students freeze tiny drops of water and observe them under the microscope. Do they resemble snowflakes?

It is often difficult of observe real snowflakes because they melt so fast. Here is one way to preserve them:

Lightly coat several glass microscope slides with a clear plastic spray found in art stores. Place the slides in a refrigerator or freezer. When the next snow falls, have students catch two or three snowflakes on a slide. Quickly spray the slide again with the clear plastic spray, being careful so as not to disturb the flakes. As the plastic dries, the shape of each flake will be preserved. Students can now examine them to their heart's content. You can even use an overhead projector to project the snowflakes' images to the entire class.

PAINTING SNOW SCENES

After reading one of the wintry books listed in the literature recommendations, ask your students to illustrate their version of the story. But, instead of white tempera paint for snow, try this mixture:

Combine in a large bowl 1 cup of Ivory Flakes, 1/3 cup liquid starch and 1/4 cup water. Beat with a wire whisk until the mixture thickens.

Use this "snow-like" paint on dark-colored paper to make truly "snowy" pictures.

ICY SPORTS

Children who live in warm climates may never give much thought to the many cold weather sports and activities that people living in cold climates regularly enjoy.

Divide the class into several groups and assign each group an icy or cold weather sport. Some ideas include ice hockey, figure skating, speed skating, downhill skiing, cross-country skiing, and bobsledding.

Each member of the group can research a different facet of the sport such as the rules, of the game, official organizations, teams, locations, individual participants or as an Olympic event.

The groups' reports can then be displayed on the class board under the name of the appropriate sport!

Winter Activities!

STORY STARTER SNOWFLAKES

With the help of your students, create a snowy mural on the class board. (Students may want to use some "snowy" paint in parts of the scene.)

Cut two or three dozen 8-inch snowflake patterns from white paper. Leave most of the center of each snowflake's hole intact. In the center of each flake write an icy story starter or three snowy words. Pin the snowflakes to the mural.

Students can choose a snowflake and write a creative winter tale using the story starter idea or the descriptive words. Here are some suggestions:

avalanche	blizzard
freeze	frostbite
hibernate	icicles
shiver	snowdrift
snowmobile	wilderness

"The skaters were skating too close to
    the thin ice!"
"It's been snowing for ten days straight!"
"We built the biggest snowman anyone
    had ever seen!"
"It snowed on the Fourth of July!"
"The champion ice skater was about to perform a jump never before attempted!"
"Oh, no! I lost my mittens again!"
"The winner of the race receives a pair of magic skates!"

MITTEN MATH

Provide your students with a pair of mittens and an indoor/outdoor thermometer for this center activity. Ask your students to complete these tasks:

1. Record the temperature indicated on the thermometer.

2. Place the bulb end of the thermometer in the palm of your hand. After three minutes, record the temperature.

3. Next, slip the mitten on and slide the bulb of the thermometer inside the mitten, resting it on the palm of your hand. After three minutes, record the temperature.

Now, answer these questions:

• What was the original temperature?
• What was the temperature after three
    minutes on the palm?
• How much did the temperature
    increase?
• What was the temperature after you
    wore the mitten?
• How much did the temperature
    increase?
• Why do you think wearing the mitten
    made the temperature warmer?

COLORFUL SNOWFLAKES

Brighten up your winter classroom with a colorful snowflake display!

Cut assorted colored tissue paper into six inch squares. Ask each student to select two or three colors and cut snowflakes shapes from each one. Have them arrange the snowflakes between two larger sheets of wax paper. Using an old sheet to protect the iron and the table top, press with a warm iron. Trim away the excess wax paper and tape thew snowflakes to the classroom windows. These colorful snow-flakes will look super from both indoors and out!

Winter Activities!

WARM UP WITH SOUP!

Have each student contribute to a hearty, class-made soup for a fun, nutritious activity. (Start the soup early in the day so it will be ready by lunch time.)

Ask each child to bring in a peeled vegetable. (Parents can do the peeling.) Provide a large pot of water, a hot plate, pot holders, salt, a ladle, a knife and bouillon cubes. Disposable bowls and spoons will also be needed. Under supervision, have the students cut their vegetable in small pieces and place the pieces in the pot of water.

Have the children measure the water and vegetables as a math exercise. They can also note the temperature of the water as it begins to boil.

(Note: The day before making the soup, review with your students the type of vegetables that taste good in soup. Assign groups of students to bring in specific vegetables. The soup won't be very tasty if, for example, the only vegetables were potatoes.)

ICE POWER

Try some of these "icy" experiments!

ICE EXPANDS Place a plastic container in the freezer and fill it to the brim with water. Lay the lid loosely on top. After the water has frozen hard, check the container and you will find the lid pushed up. Explain the properties of frozen water expansion with your students.

SALT OR SAND Which causes more traction, salt of sand? Ask children if they have ever noticed salt or sand being used for traction in icy conditions. What are the hazards of using either one?

Divide the class into groups and give each group two ice cubes and some paper towels. Ask them to sprinkle one ice cube with salt and the other with sand. Have them observe which melts the fastest. Which one creates more traction?

SALT WATER Does salt water freeze? Of course it does! It just requires a lower temperature to do so. Explain to your students how salt water in the far north or south freezes to form glaciers and icebergs. (About 10% of the world is covered with glaciers so thick they never melt.)

Prepare two glasses of salt water (one stronger than the other) and one glass of fresh water. Sit all three in the freezer and see which takes the longest to freeze.

ICICLES Show students how icicles form by using a plastic container. (A margarine tub will do.) Punch a small hole in the bottom of the container. Connect wire or heavy string so you can hang it in a tree. Fill with water on a freezing day and watch as an icicle forms.

Winter Activities!

MAKING SNOW

Make real snow in your classroom with these materials.

- 1 - 3 pound empty coffee can
- 1 - 1 pound empty coffee can
- 1 - bag of crushed ice
- 1 - small terrycloth towel
    - rock salt
    - 1/2 pound dry ice
    - sharp knife
    - masking tape

Wrap the towel around the bottom portion of the larger can and secure in place with masking tape. Put a small amount of crushed ice in the bottom of the large can and sprinkle generously with salt. (Use a ratio of about 1/3 salt to 2/3 ice.) Place the smaller can inside the larger can and continue packing the ice and salt in the space between the two cans. Fill the ice to the top of the outside of the small can.

By breathing into the small can, you can now illustrate how your breath will condense and form a cloud. This cloud is just like the clouds on a cold winter day.

Next comes the dry ice. The dry ice must be handled carefully to prevent burns. Pick the dry ice up with a cloth and scrape a few grains of ice into the cloud with a sharp knife. Ice crystals will soon start to form. Point out to the students that these crystals are just like the ones that start snowstorms in the winter. Breathe again into the small can, continuing to form the cloud. The new moisture you add with your breath will continue to freeze around the crystals, making them larger each time. Before long, your students will realize that the crystals have become real snowflakes!

ACTIVITY 1

FIND THESE WINTER WORDS IN THE PUZZLE: SNOW, ICE, MITTENS, WINTER, FROST, COLD, JACKET, SLED, ICICLE, SNOWFLAKE, SKI, SNOWMAN

Winter Word Find!

```
C M D F G S N O W M A N D R T F G T Y H J U
M D E F R G T S K I B H Y N F D R V B N M F
I G H J D F G H J G T H Y J R D T G H J K L
T D C V W I N T E R D C X Z O F T H J K L O
T D F G H J T H Y G H J K U S L E D D S A E
E M N B V C F T F C D R F C T S D A W E I K
N S D D F C G B H O J M K H V F T R D R C V
S N O W F L A K E L V C S W E S A X C Z E V
Z X C V B Y T G H D S V B N H Y U J K L T S
A S X C J A C K E T S D F V B H Y T G F E S
A S D F F G T R E C N K L M N S I C I C L E
A X D R T A C V S N O W B H Y T G F D E W S
```

Snowman Pattern

Award one pattern piece to each child as assignments are completed.

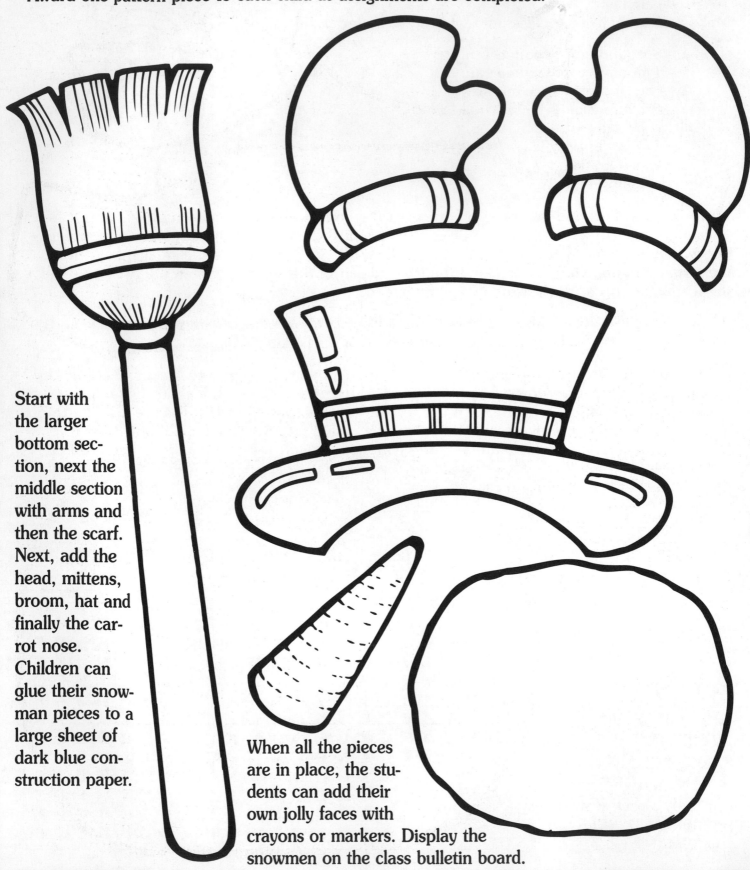

Start with the larger bottom section, next the middle section with arms and then the scarf. Next, add the head, mittens, broom, hat and finally the carrot nose. Children can glue their snowman pieces to a large sheet of dark blue construction paper.

When all the pieces are in place, the students can add their own jolly faces with crayons or markers. Display the snowmen on the class bulletin board.

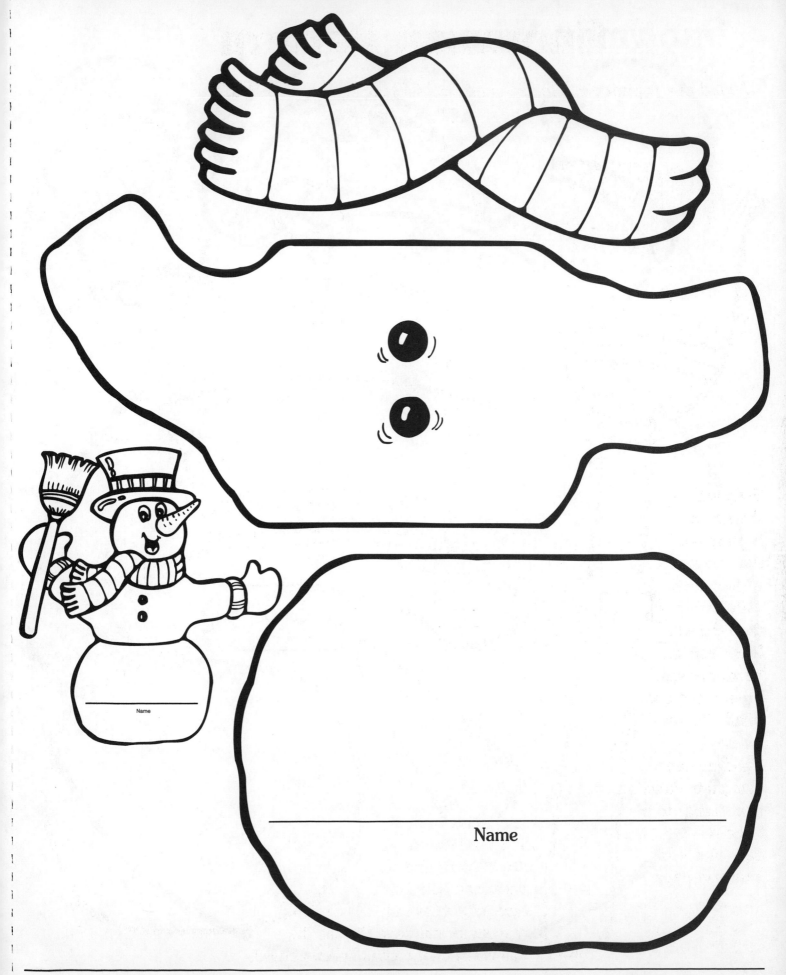

Name

Name

Snowman Wheel

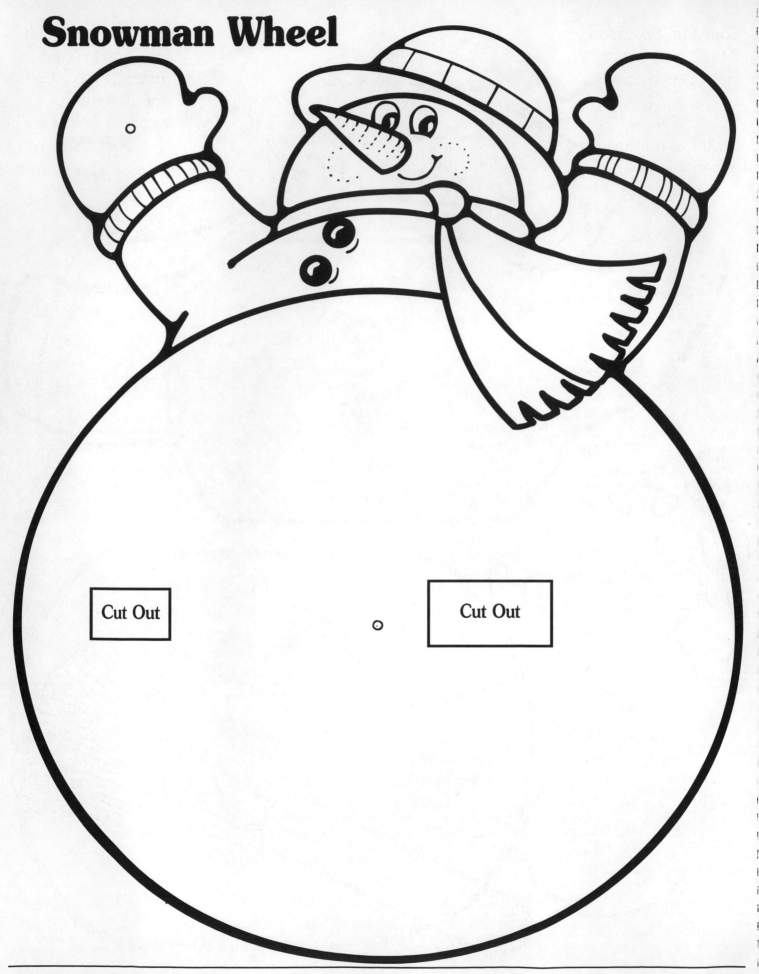

Cut Out

Cut Out

Copy the "Snowman Wheel" onto heavy index paper. Cut out and assemble with brass fasteners. Cut out the two boxes, as shown.

Add your own math problems or word contractions to the wheel. Move the broom to reveal the correct answer.

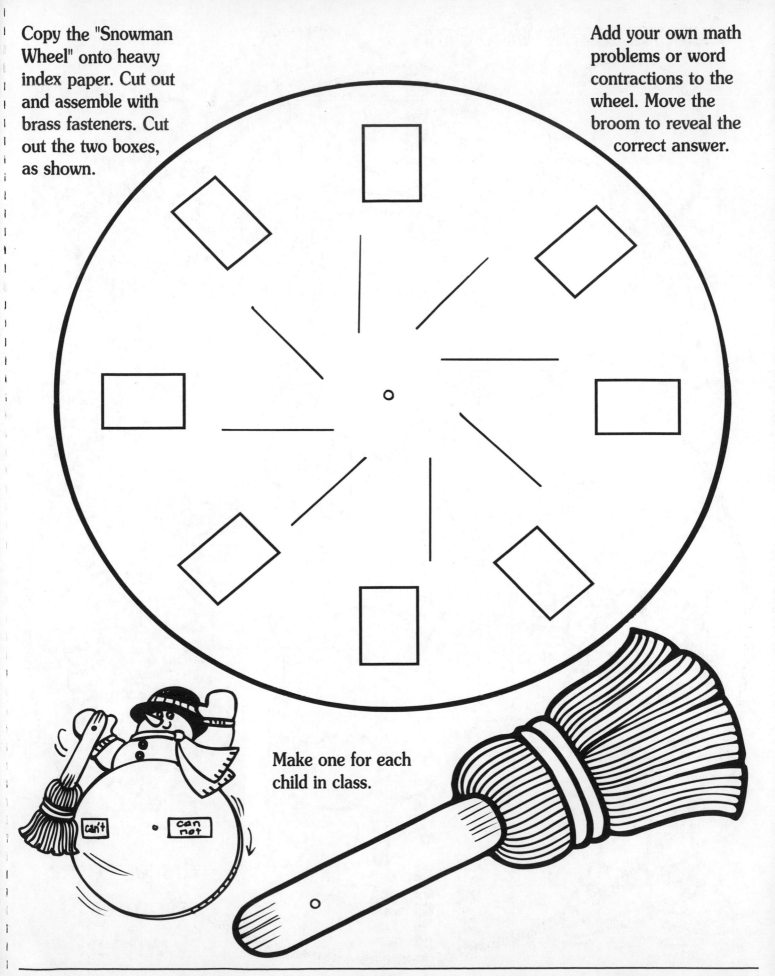

Make one for each child in class.

Warm up with a good book!

Visit the Library!

Don't Sleep All Winter...

At the Library...

discover the
wonder of
winter!

Pencil Toppers

Reproduce these "Pencil Toppers" onto construction or index paper. Color and cut out. Use an art knife to cut through the Xs.

Slide a pencil through both Xs, as shown.

Shawn!

Give them as classroom awards or birthday treats.

_____
Name

is having a great year!

Date
_____

Teacher
_____

_____
Name

Really Tried Hard Today!

Date
_____

Teacher
_____

_____
Name

was a real joy in class today!

Date
_____

Teacher
_____

_____
Name

was a BIG help today!

Date
_____

Teacher
_____

STUDENT
OF THE
WEEK

NAME

SCHOOL

DATE

TEACHER

AWARD CERTIFICATE

presented to

NAME

in recognition of

TEACHER

DATE

Girl Skater

Cut this skater pattern from construction or index paper and assemble with brass fasteners.

Children can decorate the costume.

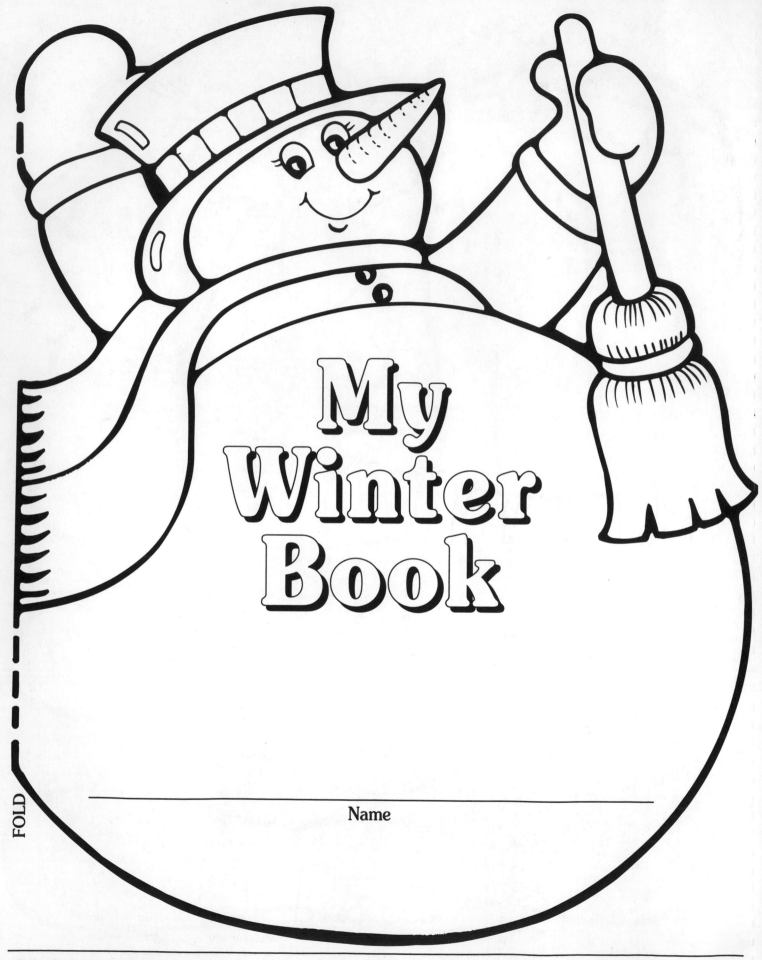

My
Winter
Book

_____
Name

TF0100 January Idea Book

Around the Year!

39

Calendar Activities!

Try one of these calendar activities when teaching the concepts of time and the seasons.

GREGORIAN CALENDAR

The calendar that most of the world uses today is called the Gregorian Calendar, named after Pope Gregory XIII, who declared its use in 1582.

The Gregorian calendar is based upon the time it takes for the earth to make one complete revolution around the sun, which is 365 days, 5 hours and 48 minutes. The extra minutes eventually add up to an extra day. So, every four years we add it to the end of the month of February (Leap Year).

Let children make their own monthly or yearly calendars. Instruct them to write in the name of the month and the numbers on the appropriate days. Tell them to also label holidays and family birthdays. These calendars make excellent gifts for Christmas or the New Year.

(There is a blank calendar page appropriate for each month in every Teacher's Friend Monthly Idea Book.)

MINUTES, HOURS, DAYS...

Ask your students to complete the following statements on the class board:

- There are _____ seconds in an hour.
- There are _____ hours in an day.
- There are _____ days in a week.
- There are _____ weeks in a month.
- There are _____ months in a year.
- There are _____ years in a century.

Now, ask them to compute how many seconds in a week, how many days in a year, etc.

MONTH BY MONTH

Create a variety of matching and organizational activities using the cards provided in this unit.

Reproduce the cards for all students onto heavy paper and ask them to color and cut them out. Have students complete some of the following:

- Place the seasons in order.
- Place the names of the days in order.
- Place the months in order.
- Group all the seasonal symbols together.
- Put the monthly names in alphabetical order.
- Put the days of the week in alphabetical order.
- Group together all the months with 30 days and those with 31 days. Which month has fewer than 30 days?

The game of "Concentration" can also be played with the cards. With a partner, students turn two decks of cards upside down. Turn over two cards. If the seasons match, keep the cards. If they don't match, turn them back over and lose a turn. Continue the game to see who wins the most cards. Now, play the game with days of the week or month.

YEARLY FAVORITES

Ask children to think about their favorite time of year or month and write about it in the form of a poem or short story.

Ask them also to tell if they have a favorite day of the week. Instruct them to list all of their reasons for choosing this particular day.

Months of the Year!

WORD FIND - ACTIVITY 2

FIND THE MONTHS OF THE YEAR IN THE PUZZLE BELOW: JANUARY, FEBRUARY, MARCH, APRIL, MAY, JUNE, JULY, AUGUST, SEPTEMBER, OCTOBER, NOVEMBER, DECEMBER.

```
A M S D F R E T G D C Q A S E D F R G B N M C D S J
A X C M A R C H A C F V B G H N J U N E O U K I G A
A S S D E F R T G J S D E R T G B N H J U K I L I N
P S D S E P T E M B E R F G H Y J U K I O L G T D U
R D F G T H Y J U D F R T G H Y N J U G C H Y U G A
I S W E D C V G T D E C E M B E R D R F T S W A W R
L S X C V B G F D S A W E R T G Y A D E O F R S E Y
X S A F R E T Y H G T R E D C F G T R A B R G H J S
G J U L Y A X M Z S E R C V G Y H Y A R E F G V B N
X Z C V B G T A A N O V E M B E R K L E R A S E D F
A W S D F R C Y A S D C V F G D C V F G A U G U S T
A S X F E B R U A R Y C V B H J K L O P M N G F D S
```

ACTIVITY 3

BDREECEM _____

TUUSGA _____

CMRAH _____

TEROOCB _____

RYUABRFE _____

NEUJ _____

RLPAI _____

VMEONREB _____

AMY _____

UYNJAAR _____

PMEESRBET _____

LJYU _____

Now, unscramble the months!

Desktop Calendar

Have each of your students make his or her own desktop calendar with these patterns.

Color and cut out each pattern piece. Cut out the three indicated windows. Fold along the dotted line and attach the wheels inside the calendar using brass fasteners.

Each morning, students turn the wheels to the appropriate month and day. As the seasons change have them move the season wheel.

This desktop calendar makes a great parent gift, as well!

DAY

Cut Out

SEASON

Cut out

MY

CALENDAR

Year

Student's Name

MONTH

Cut Out

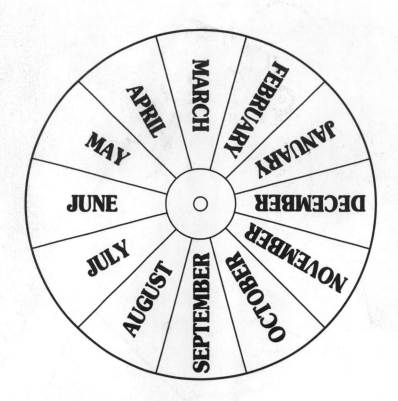

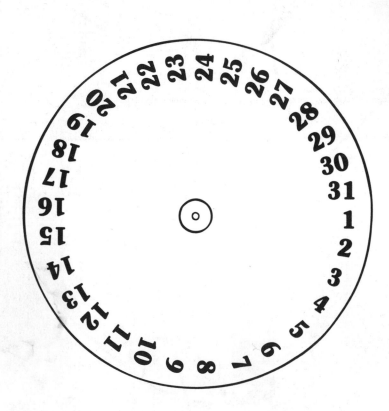

You may want to enlarge each of the Desktop Calendar Patterns and use them on a bulletin board as a classroom calendar. Assign students to change the wheels daily.

My
Book of
Months

_____
Name

January

January is the _____ month.

January has _____ days.

These people have birthdays in January:

_____   _____

_____   _____

_____

Here are four words that describe January:

1. _____   3. _____

2. _____   4. _____

I like January because: _____

_____

_____

_____

My favorite holiday in January is: _____

_____

(On another piece of paper write a poem about the weather in January.)

February

February is the _____ month.

February has _____ days.

These people have birthdays in February:

_____   _____

_____   _____

_____   _____

Here are four words that describe February:

1. _____   3. _____

2. _____   4. _____

I like February because: _____

_____

_____

_____

My favorite holiday in February is: _____

_____

(On another piece of paper write a story about a groundhog
who forgot to look for his shadow.)

March

March is the _____ month.

March has _____ days.

These people have birthdays in March:

_____   _____

_____   _____

_____   _____

Here are four words that describe March:

1. _____   3. _____

2. _____   4. _____

I like March because: _____

_____

_____

_____

My favorite holiday in March is: _____

_____

(On another piece of paper write a riddle about a leprechaun and
share it with a friend.)

April

April is the _____ month.

April has _____ days.

These people have birthdays in April:

_____   _____

_____   _____

_____   _____

Here are four words that describe April:

1. _____   3. _____

2. _____   4. _____

I like April because: _____

_____

_____

_____

My favorite holiday in April is: _____

_____

(On another piece of paper write a poem about April showers.)

May

May is the _____ month.

May has _____ days.

These people have birthdays in May:

_____ _____

_____ _____

_____

Here are four words that describe May:

1. _____ 3. _____

2. _____ 4. _____

I like May because: _____

_____

_____

My favorite holiday in May is: _____

_____

(On another piece of paper write a loving note to your mom and give
it to her on Mother's Day.)

June

June is the _____ month.

June has _____ days.

These people have birthdays in June:

_____   _____

_____   _____

_____

Here are four words that describe June:

1. _____   3. _____

2. _____   4. _____

I like June because: _____

_____

_____

My favorite holiday in June is: _____

_____

(On another piece of paper make a list of the reasons you love
and appreciate your dad and give it to him on Father's Day.)

July

July is the _____ month.

July has _____ days.

These people have birthdays in July:

_____   _____

_____   _____

_____   _____

Here are four words that describe July:

1. _____   3. _____

2. _____   4. _____

I like July because: _____

_____

_____

_____

My favorite holiday in July is: _____

_____

(On another piece of paper write a list of the many things you'd
like to eat at a Fourth of July picnic.)

                                       TF0100 January Idea Book

August

August is the _____ month.

August has _____ days.

These people have birthdays in August:

_____   _____

_____   _____

_____   _____

Here are four words that describe August:

1. _____   3. _____

2. _____   4. _____

I like August because: _____

_____

_____

_____

My favorite holiday in August is: _____

_____

(Take a few minutes to look at the night sky and write a story
about your thoughts on another piece of paper write.)

September

September is the _____ month.

September has _____ days.

These people have birthdays in September:

_____   _____

_____   _____

Here are four words that describe September:

1. _____   3. _____

2. _____   4. _____

I like September because: _____

_____

_____

_____

My favorite holiday in September is: _____

_____

(On another piece of paper write about the things you would
most wish to learn during the coming school year.)

October

October is the _____ month.

October has _____ days.

These people have birthdays in October:

_____ _____

_____ _____

_____ _____

Here are four words that describe October:

1. _____ 3. _____

2. _____ 4. _____

I like October because: _____

_____

_____

_____

My favorite holiday in October is: _____

_____

(On another piece of paper write a spooky poem
about the Halloween holiday.)

November

November is the _____ month.

November has _____ days.

These people have birthdays in November:

_____   _____

_____   _____

_____

Here are four words that describe November:

1. _____   3. _____

2. _____   4. _____

I like November because: _____

_____

_____

_____

My favorite holiday in November is: _____

_____

(On another piece of paper write a recipe for roasting
a turkey including the stuffing.)

     TF0100 January Idea Book

December

December is the _____ month.

December has _____ days.

These people have birthdays in December:

_____ _____

_____ _____

_____ _____

Here are four words that describe December:

1. _____ 3. _____

2. _____ 4. _____

I like December because: _____

_____

_____

_____

My favorite holiday in December is: _____

_____

(On another piece of paper write make a list of gifts you can give during
the holiday season that cost no money.)

Monthly Symbols

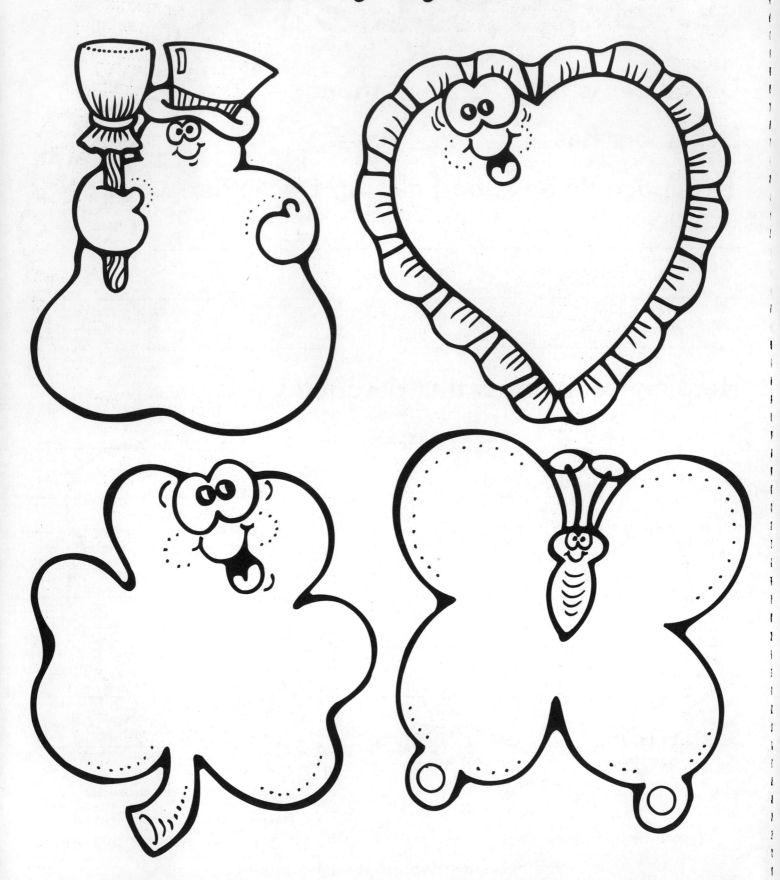

Dress Me!

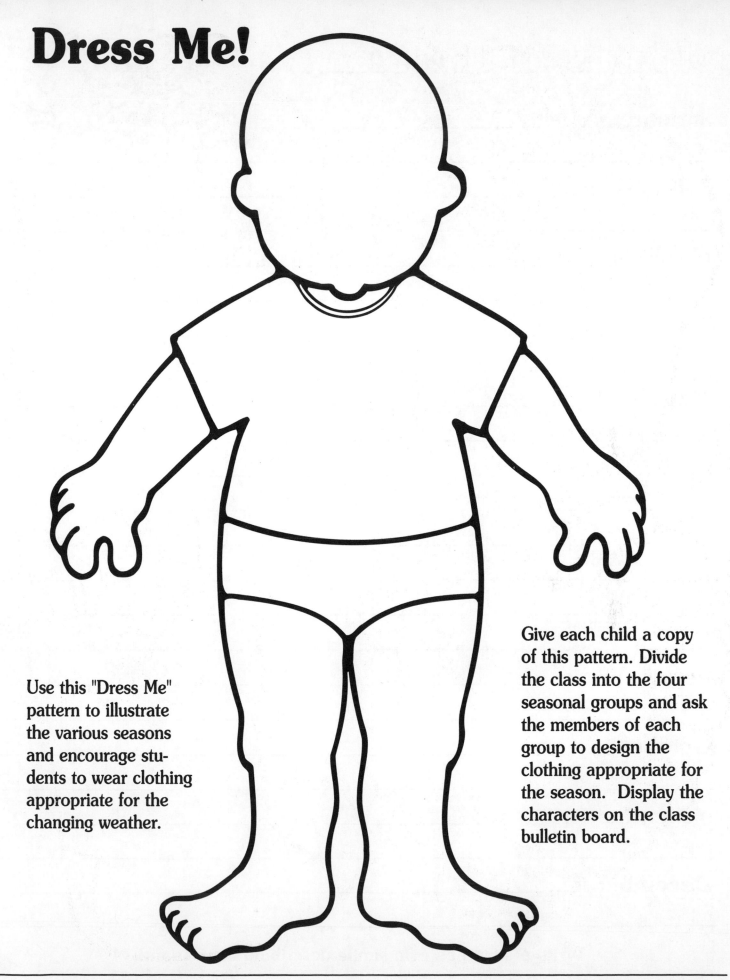

Use this "Dress Me" pattern to illustrate the various seasons and encourage students to wear clothing appropriate for the changing weather.

Give each child a copy of this pattern. Divide the class into the four seasonal groups and ask the members of each group to design the clothing appropriate for the season. Display the characters on the class bulletin board.

Months of the Year...

January is... _____

_____

February is... _____

_____

March is... _____

_____

April is... _____

_____

May is... _____

_____

June is... _____

_____

July is... _____

_____

August is... _____

_____

September is... _____

_____

October is... _____

_____

November is... _____

_____

December is... _____

_____

Write a sentence or a simile describing each month.

New Year's Day!

New Year's Day - January 1st!

The custom of celebrating the New Year on January 1st began over 2,000 years ago in Rome, Italy. The Romans had previously celebrated March 25th, the vernal equinox, as the beginning of the New Year. Government officials were elected in December and assumed their new positions on the day before January 1st. Gradually, citizens began celebrating this first day as the beginning of the New Year. This change, however, created confusion in the Roman calendar. The months of September, October, November and December, (which refer to the seventh, eighth, ninth and tenth months of the year) were now the ninth, tenth, eleventh and twelfth month. By changing the New Year to January, these month's names had little meaning.

In 45 B.C., Roman emperor Julius Caesar selected the name "January" for the first month of the year. This name was chosen to honor the Roman god Janus. It was believed that this god had two faces each looking in opposite directions. In his right hand he held a key to unlock the door to the future and guard the door to the past. In his left hand he held a scepter as a symbol of authority. The Senate of Rome awarded Julius Caesar a month of his own for his successful transfer of the New Year and his improvement on the Roman Calendar. We now call this month "July."

Today, people of diffferent countries celebrate New Year's Day in a variety of ways.

GERMANY - The people of Germany enjoy a custom called "lead pouring." On New Year's Day, youngsters drop hot drops of melted lead into containers of cold water. As the lead cools and hardens, unusual shapes appear. The children have fun telling their fortunes by the shapes of the lead. According to custom, if the lead shape resembles a coin, they might look forward to obtaining money.

ROSH HASHANA - The Jewish New Year provides a quiet time for meditation and prayer. This is a holy date to the Jewish people, considered the birthday of the world. Each person asks forgiveness from God and vows to live a better life. Rosh Hashana is celebrated on the first day of the Jewish calendar, in September or October.

SWEDEN - The Swedish people celebrate the New Year with parties and family gatherings on the last night of the year. There is much food and merrymaking and friendship and good wishes are expressed to one and all.

AUSTRIA - Ever since 1936, the Austrian government has commemorated the New Year with the minting of good luck tokens called "Gluecksmenze." New Year wishes are engraved on one side of the coin and good luck symbols on the other. Austrians also enjoy eating New Year's candies in the shape of good-luck pigs.

NIGERIA - The people of northern Nigeria celebrate the New Year at the beginning of fishing season, usually the first part of February. Thousands of people gather along the banks of the Sokoto River with fish nets in hand. At a given signal, everyone jumps in the water, startling the fish into the nets. The fisherman with the largest fish wins a prize.

New Year's Day - January 1st!

SOUTHERN UNITED STATES - It is a Southern tradition to serve black-eyed peas on New Year's Day for good luck! Prepare the peas the night before by soaking them in a pot of water. In the morning, rinse the peas and place them in a Crock-Pot® covered with water. Add a chopped onion, salt pork and some salt and pepper. Set the pot to cook on high all day in the classroom. When the peas are tender, serve a portion to each student.

SEMINOLE NEW YEAR - For four days during the month of July, the Seminole Indians of Florida celebrate the harvest of new corn as the beginning of the New Year. On the first day, they play games, feast and dance. On the second day, the men of the tribe begin a fast. Everyone dances the Green Corn Dance on the third evening and gives prayers of thanks for the good harvest. Finally, on the last day, the men break their fast and eat the new corn of the New Year.

UNITED STATES - In our country, the old year is symbolized by an old man, Father Time, and the New Year is represented by a baby in diapers. In the southern states, it is customary to eat certain foods on New Year's Day in hopes of bringing prosperity through the coming year. Black-eyed peas symbolize pennies and greens represent dollar bills. Making New Year's resolutions is a relatively new custom based on the idea of improving the New Year in the hope that it will be better than the last.

New Year's Day Word Find!

ACTIVITY 4

FIND THESE NEW YEAR WORDS IN THE PUZZLE BELOW: JANUARY, NEW YEAR, BELLS, CELEBRATE, MIDNIGHT, FATHER TIME, RESOLUTION, CONFETTI, BALLOONS, CUSTOM, FRIENDS.

```
G N M K L O P L K M J N H G A S W E R T X
A S W D V F R T F V G E S E D F T G H Y U
F R I E N D S X D R T W U I C F T G B N B
Q E S D F R G T G H N Y F R C U S T O M N
A S E R C V B N H Y T E W S C V F R G D J
A O C V B C O N D V F A F R B D E R T Y Y
X L C O N F E T T I D R S E E C V B N M I
Q U X C V B G F D E B A E F L A S D E R U
A T D F G H X E R T Y H C E L E B R A T E
Z I X C V G T F R E D F G T S D V B N M U
A O F B N M J K F A T H E R T I M E X C T
W N S D B A L L O O N S C D R E T G H Y N
M I D N I G H T V D E R T F G R D S W E R
A S D E W Q X C V J A N U A R Y N H J K L
```

My New Year's Resolutions!

Name _____

During New Year's celebrations, we often pledge to make the coming year better than the last. Many people make New Year's resolutions. Think of some resolutions you want to make and write them in the spaces below.

List your resolution for becoming a better...

Student _____

_____

Son or Daughter _____

_____

Sister of Brother _____

_____

Friend _____

_____

If you could make one New Year's resolution for our country or the world, what would it be?

_____

_____

_____

Write your own resolutions
in your New Year Book.

Happy New Year Visor

Copy this "Happy New Year" visor onto sturdy index or construction paper. Children can do the coloring.

Punch holes at both ends and attach string elastic or mailing string. (With elastic, the students can easily remove the visors without retying.)

Wishful Thinking!

Most students have wishes and goals for the new year. Encourage their creative thinking by suggesting some of these activities.

SECRET WISHES

Add an element of mystery to your next creative writing assignment with this simple idea.

Ask students to write a sentence describing a secret wish on white paper using a white crayon. (The wish will appear to be invisible.) Collect all the papers and then redistribute them, making sure no one receives their own paper back.

The students then paint over the messages with watercolors to reveal their secret wishes. Instruct the children to write short stories including the secret wishes.

CREATIVE WISHES

Write a variety of special wishes on numerous clouds cut from white construction paper. Place the clouds in a "magic" box someplace in the classroom. (Cover the "magic" box with metallic paper and decorate with lightning bolts, stars and moons.)

When a child has finished his or her work, he ir she may pull out a cloud and write a story using the "wishful" suggestions. Here are some ideas:

"I wish I could ride a magic
   carpet!"
"I wish money grew on trees!"
"I wish every day was Saturday!"
"I wish candy bars were good for you!"
"I wish there was really a pot of gold
   at the end of every rainbow!"

WISHES CAN COME TRUE!

Discuss with your class how wishes can come true. Ask them to brainstorm the idea and list the suggestions on the class board.

Begin by explaining that with effort and hard work, many wishes can come true. For example, if someone wishes for good grades the wish can come true by having good study habits. Another example might be a person wishing for a good friend can begin by being friendly and kind to others.

MAGIC WANDS

Children will love making their own personal magic wand!

Cut stars from gold or silver metallic paper, two for each student. Give each student an 18" dowel and ask them to cover it with strips of colored tissue paper. (Real ribbon, lace, sequins, etc. can be added.) Streamers of tissue paper can be added to the top of the dowel. When the tissue paper is dry, glue the stars, back to back, to the top of the dowel.

The magic wands can now be used in role playing. Select groups of two students to act out various scenarios related to granting wishes. If the wish is unselfish, it may be granted. If it is selfish, it will be denied.

You might like to use a magic wand in the classroom to excuse quiet or obedient students to recess.

Wishful Thinking!

MAKE-A-WISH

At the beginning of the school year, enlist the help of your students in saving pennies for a worthy charity. This activity will provide endless opportunities for math computations as well as a valuable way to teach the joys of sharing.

Instruct students to bring pennies from home or pick them up when found on the ground. The pennies can then be counted and rolled by the students when work is completed.

You may want to notify parents of the activity before you start. You will also need to provide a safe place for the rolled pennies in the classroom.

An excellent charity to select might be:

    Make-a-Wish Foundation
    100 W. Clarendon, Suite 2200
    Phoenix, AZ 85013
    Phone: (800) 722-9474

This charity literally makes wishes come true for terminally ill children.

WREATH OF WORLD WISHES

Inspire children to think of ways to help the world and its inhabitants can be helped, with this crafty idea.

Cut a large ring from poster board. Ask each child to trace and cut out his or her right hand on colored construction paper. (Use a variety of different colors.) Instruct the children to write their "Wishes for the World" on the hands. Glue the hands slightly overlapping around the ring. Paste a large paper bow to the top of the wreath and ask each child to sign it with his or her name. Display the wreath in the classroom during the holidays, or anytime during year!

WHEN YOU WISH UPON A STAR!

Give students large paper stars on which to write their wishes for the year ahead. Pin the stars to the class board that has been covered with dark blue or black butcher paper. Entitle the board "When You Wish Upon a Star!"

Save the stars until the end of the school year and distribute them to the students at that time. Let each child tell the rest of the class whether his or her wish came true.

DOG

1958, 1970, 1982, 1994, 2006,

Those born under the Dog sign are extremely loyal and honest. They have a deep sense of justice and duty and can always keep a secret.

BOAR

1959, 1971, 1983, 1995, 2007

People born under this sign have a strong inner strength and are very brave. They are shy, courteous and make friends for life.

RAT

1960, 1972, 1984, 1996, 2008

People born under the sign of the Rat have great charm. They are known for their ambition, integrity and drive.

OX

1961, 1973, 1985, 1997, 2009

OX people are very patient and are good listeners. They inspire others with their calm assuredness.

TIGER

Tiger people are considered very good friends. They are careful planners and are respected by others.

1962, 1974, 1986, 1998, 2010

HARE

Persons born under the sign of the hare are blessed with good fortune and seldom lose their tempers. They always keep their promises.

1963, 1975, 1987, 1999, 2011

DRAGON

People born under the sign of the Dragon have been given the gifts of courage, health and gentleness. They are good rulers and sensitive to others.

1952, 1964, 1976, 1988, 2012

SNAKE

People born under this sign possess great wisdom. They are fortunate in money matters and are very handsome or beautiful.

1953, 1965, 1977, 1989, 2001

HORSE

Those born under the sign of the Horse are very cheerful and popular with others. They are good with their hands and quite talented.

1954, 1966, 1978, 1990, 2002

RAM

People born under this sign are very artistic and enjoy beautiful things. They are most happy when doing creative tasks.

1955, 1967, 1979, 1991, 2003

MONKEY

Monkey people are good decision makers and great common sense. They are quite successful and keep themselves well-informed.

1956, 1968, 1980, 1992, 2004

ROOSTER

People born under this sign are outspoken and deep thinkers. They are devoted to their work and attract loyal friends.

1957, 1969, 1981, 1993, 2005

Fish Kite

These gorgeous Fish Kites are fun to run with in the wind and make a beautiful bulletin board display.

Copy the fish pattern onto colored typing paper and have each student cut two patterns. (You may want to enlarge the pattern for larger fish kites.)

Students can staple or glue the edges of their two fish shapes together, leaving the tail and mouth open. Children will love decorating their kites with crayons, paints, glitter and markers. Crepe paper streamers can also be added.

Fold the mouth of the kite inward a few of times and shape it into a round opening. Attach kite string or yarn to the opening, as shown.

Chinese Food!

CHOPSTICKS
Place one chopstick firmly between the forefinger and thumb. Move the top stick up and down against the lower stick to grasp food.

SCRAMBLED CHINESE EGGS
Heat 2 tablespoons of oil and saute 1/2 minced onion in a frying pan or wok. Beat six or eight eggs with 2 teaspoons of soy sauce and add to the onions. Stir over medium heat until the eggs are cooked. Serve with stir-fried snowpeas, bean sprouts and bamboo shoots.

The main food in the Chinese diet is rice. Prepare enough rice for everyone in class and serve it in paper cups with chopsticks. (Many grocery stores carry disposable chopsticks in economical packages.)

STIR FRY VEGETABLES
Bring an electric skillet or a Chinese wok and portable hot plate to the classroom. Let the students cut a variety of vegetables such as celery, bok choy, onions, bean sprouts and water chesnuts. Heat a small amount of vegetable oil in the skillet and saute the vegetables. (Do not overcook.) Serve this healthy food to your students with soy sauce.

You may also like to prepare white rice in a rice cooker. Serve the vegetables over the rice. A yummy treat even non-vegetable eaters will enjoy!

FORTUNE COOKIES
Chinese Fortune Cookies are easy to make and especially fun during Chinese New Year celebrations.

Begin by asking each student to write a fortune or saying on a small strip of typing paper and fold in half.

Assign two or three students to measure the following ingredients:

8 egg whites	2 cups sugar
1 cup melted butter	1 cup flour
1 teaspoon vanilla	1/2 teaspoon salt
4 tablespoons water	

Separate the egg whites and beat them until they form stiff peaks. Blend in the sugar and butter. Discard the yolks. Add the flour, vanilla, salt and water to the mixture and mix until it is smooth. Grease a cookie sheet and spoon the batter into 3 inch circles. Bake at 375° for about 3 minutes.

When the cookies are done, remove them with a pancake turner onto waxed paper. Place a fortune in the center of each circle and fold the cookie in half. Bend the cookies gently in the center, as shown. (If the cookies become difficult to bend, put them back in the oven for a minute or so.)

Children will be delighted to select a cookie and read their special fortune written by a fellow classmate.

Note: The recipe does not work well with microwave ovens.

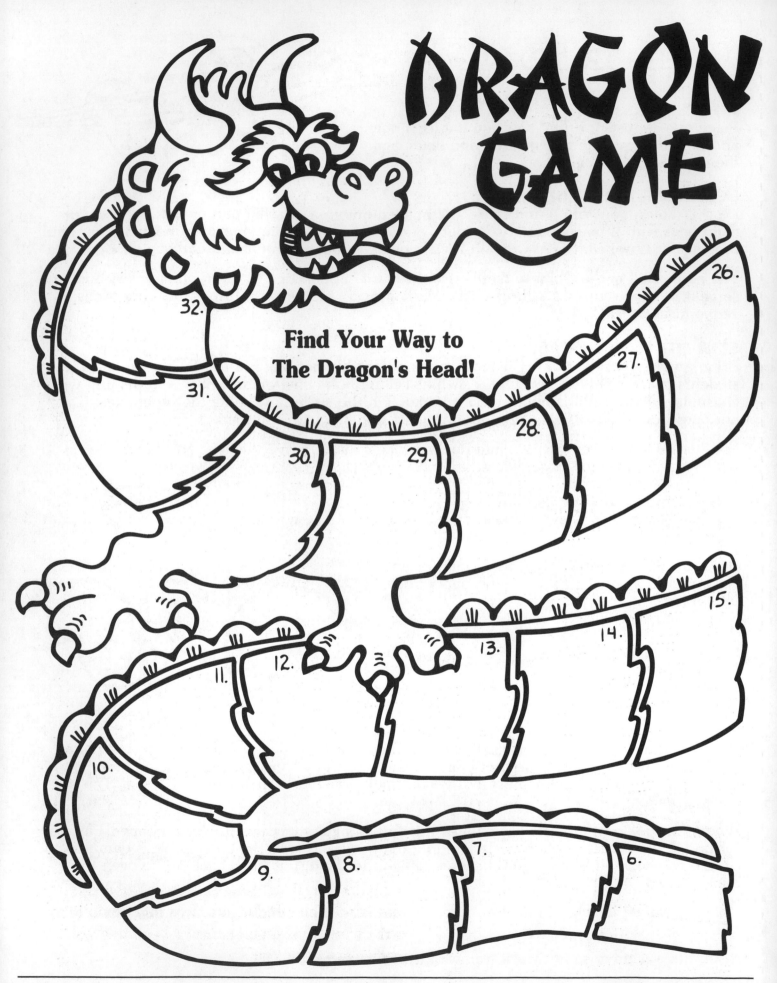

DRAGON GAME

Find Your Way to The Dragon's Head!

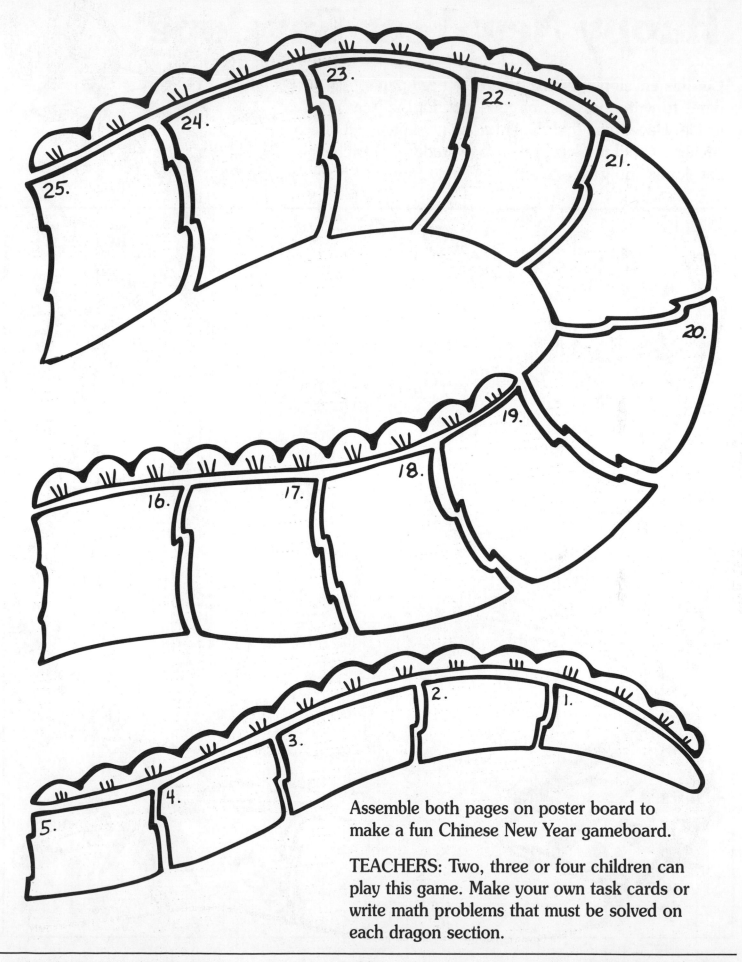

Assemble both pages on poster board to make a fun Chinese New Year gameboard.

TEACHERS: Two, three or four children can play this game. Make your own task cards or write math problems that must be solved on each dragon section.

Happy N w Y ar Env lope

Cut this envelope pattern from bright red paper. Ask students to write messages of good luck for the New Year inside. Have them fold the envelope as shown and attach a sticker to hold in place. Encourage students to exchange envelopes and wish one another "Gung Hey Fat Choy!"

Happy New Year Banner

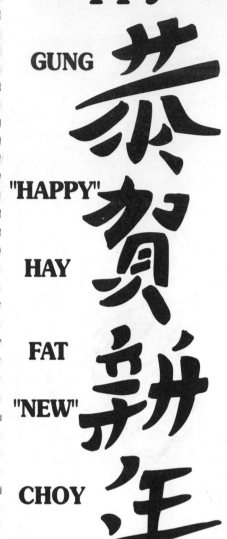

GUNG

"HAPPY"

HAY

FAT

"NEW"

CHOY

"YEAR"

Children will love speaking and writing Chinese during Chinese New Year celebrations. Ask students to pronounce the words "Kung Shi" (Gung She) which means "Happy New Year." Traditionally, this greeting is said to friendswhile bowed at the waist with hands folded. After the children have perfected their greeting, have them try their hand at writing the characters "Gung Hay Fat Choy" on New Year banners.

Cut long rectangles, about 12" x 30", of red butcher paper and ask students to write the characters "Gung Hay Fat Choy" down the center of the banners with black tempera paint.

After the banners have dried, cut 12" strips of black construction paper. Fold the strips over long pieces of yarn and staple to the top of the banners.

Hang these lovely Chinese greetings in your classroom throughout your New Year celebrations.

Lantern

Make dozens of Chinese lanterns simply by having each student fold a 12" x 18" sheet of colored construction paper in half and cut as shown. Ask them to unfold the paper and staple the outside edges to form a cylinder. Students can add paper handles and cut-paper decorations if they wish. Hang them throughout your classroom for a truly festive atmosphere.

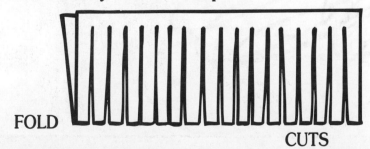

FOLD

CUTS

International Children

China

84

International Children

China

Tangram

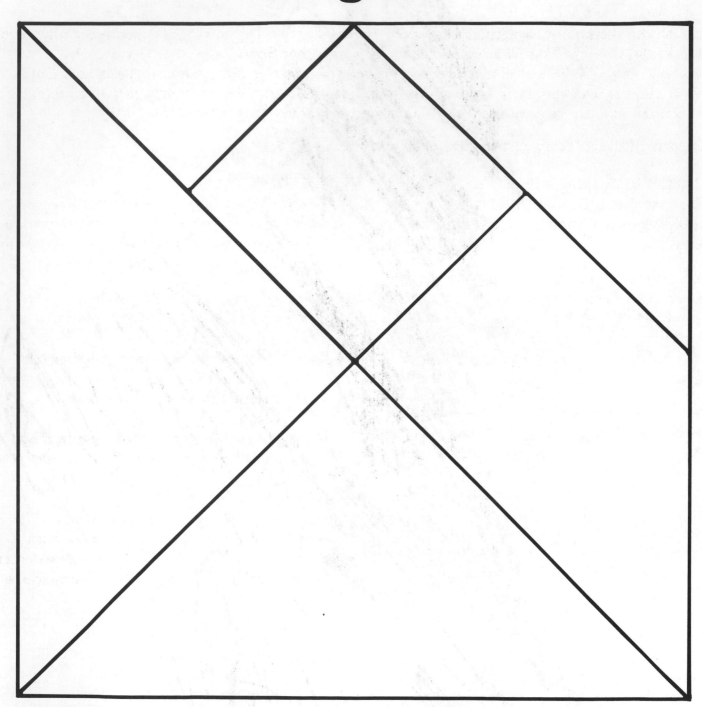

A Tangram is an ancient Chinese puzzle cut from a square piece of paper. It consists of five triangles, a parallelogram and a small square. These seven shapes can be combined to form many different shapes and designs.

Give each of your students a copy of the Tangram. Have them cut out the pieces and arrange them on a contrasting colored sheet of paper. Glue the shapes in place and display the best Tangrams on the class board.

Chinese Dragon Activities!

In Chinese mythology, dragons play a very important role. Dragon themes are especially used during the Chinese New Year celebrations. It is said that Shen Lung, the "Good Luck Dragon", is the mightiest of all dragons. He controls the sea, sky, moon, sun and soil. But Shen Lung is also very lazy. Legend says that he avoids work by shrinking himself to the size of a small mouse. As a mouse, he hides in people's houses for most of the year.

Try one of these "Dragon" activities with your students.

CATCH THE DRAGON'S TAIL

This energetic, outside game will give your kids a vigorous workout and a lot of laughs, too!

Ask your students to form one long line. Have them each put his or her hands on the shoulders of the child in front. The first student in line is called the "Dragon's Head," and the last student is called the "Dragon's Tail."

Tell the "Dragon's Head" that he or she must catch the "Dragon's Tail." This isn't as easy as you might think, because the line must twist and turn to follow the "Head," but at the same time each student must not lose hold of the student before him or her. When the "Head" catches the "Tail," the two students switch positions. Let the children have turns being the "Dragon's Head."

DRAGON TALES

There are few better ways to tap into the creativity of a youngster's imagination than with the theme of "dragons!" Here are a few suggestions for "dragon" story starters!

• List 10 ways to catch a dragon.
• Tell about the day a dragon went shopping.
• Write an advertisement for a babysitter for your pet dragon.
• Write directions for giving a dragon a bath.
• Tell about the dragon who tried to stop smoking.

DESCRIPTIVE DRAGONS

Ask your students to describe what a dragon would be like, if there were such a thing! You may want to write the descriptive statements on the class board. Some ideas might include:

Bigger than a house.
Has horns and wings.
Breathes fire and smoke.
Is purple with spots.
Can fly away.
Lives in a cave.
Can disappear.
Has a long, pointed tail.

When the class has discussed every possible description of a dragon, ask students to draw a picture of the dragon using all of the descriptions. Instruct the students to each write a story about their imaginary dragon.

Dragon Display

For a fantastic bulletin board display, enlarge these dragon head and claws patterns using heavy paper. Color with brightly colored markers or crayons. (Make several copies of the feet.)

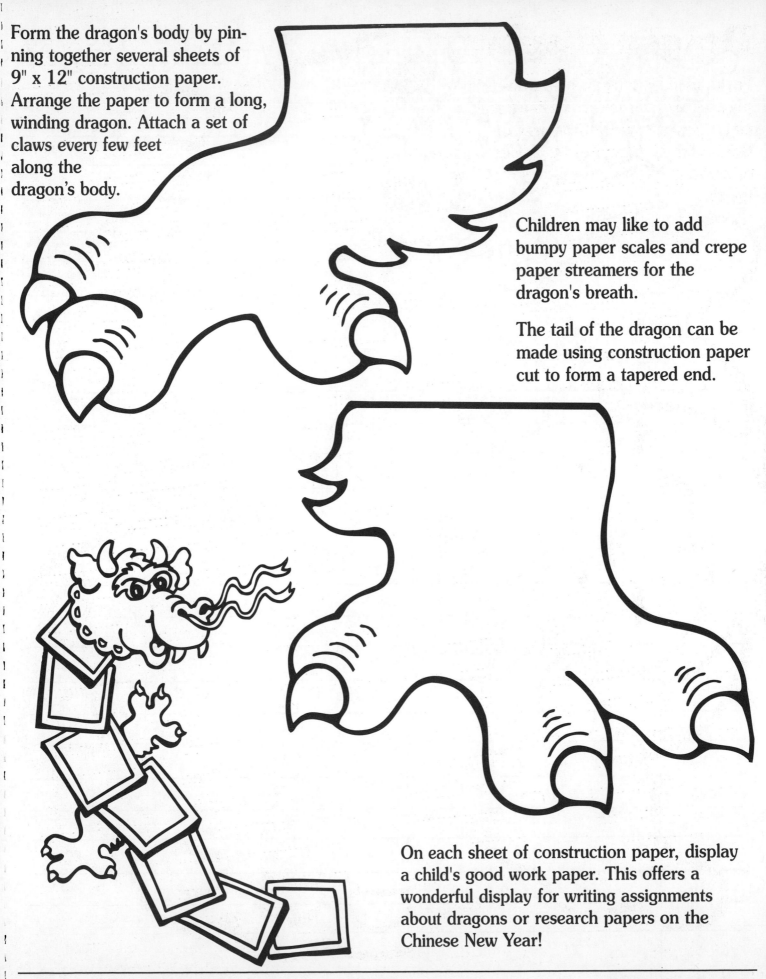

Form the dragon's body by pinning together several sheets of 9" x 12" construction paper. Arrange the paper to form a long, winding dragon. Attach a set of claws every few feet along the dragon's body.

Children may like to add bumpy paper scales and crepe paper streamers for the dragon's breath.

The tail of the dragon can be made using construction paper cut to form a tapered end.

On each sheet of construction paper, display a child's good work paper. This offers a wonderful display for writing assignments about dragons or research papers on the Chinese New Year!

Creative Writing Page!

Dr. Martin Luther King, Jr.

Martin Luther King Day - Jan. 15th!

Few in the history of Black America have inspired a nation as did Dr. Martin Luther King, Jr. He has been one of the country's most dynamic leaders in the fight for peaceful equality of all individuals.

Martin Luther King was born on January 15, 1929 in Atlanta, Georgia. His father was a well-known minister of one of Atlanta's leading black churches. In 1947, he was ordained a Baptist minister and later accepted the pastorship of Dexter Avenue Baptist church in Montgomery, Alabama. In 1953, he married Coretta Scott and together they raised four children.

During the 1950's, Martin Luther King became a leader in the Civil Rights Movement overtaking the South. His first challenge was the boycotting of segregated buses in Montgomery, Alabama. Rosa Parks, a black seamstress, refused to give up her bus seat to a white passenger. The arrest of Mrs. Parks triggered the 382-day boycott by black passengers. Many of the whites blamed Dr. King for the success of the boycott and threats on his life became very real when a bomb exploded on his family's front porch. However, Dr. King stood fast in his conviction of non-violence and urged his people to forgive their enemies and achieve a peaceful solution to their problems. The bus boycott was recognized as a clear victory for nonviolent protest and Dr. King was regarded as a highly respected leader in the movement.

Dr. King took part in many marches and demonstrations. A huge civil rights movement in Birmingham, Alabama was followed by major drives for black voter registration. By 1967, Dr. King had been arrested and jailed thirteen times for his peaceful demonstrations.

On August 28, 1963, a massive civil rights demonstration was held in front of the Lincoln Memorial in Washington, D.C. Dr. King spoke to more than 250,000 people about his "dream." This is the most famous excerpt from his speech:

"I have a dream that one day this nation will rise up and live out the true meaning of its creed: 'We hold these truths to be self-evident, that all men are created equal.'"

"I have a dream that one day on the red hills of Georgia the sons of former slaves and the sons of former slave owners will be able to sit down together at the table of brotherhood. I have a dream that one day even the state of Mississippi, a state sweltering with the heat of oppression, will be transformed into an oasis of freedom and justice."

"I have a dream that my four little children will one day live in a nation where they will not be judged by the color of their skin but by the content of their character..."

Martin Luther King Day - Jan. 15th!

President Kennedy presented the Civil Rights Bill to Congress in 1963. With the passage of this bill, Black American at last had a foothold on the road to freedom. With this bill and the Voting Rights Act, American Blacks began receiving the opportunities they needed in employment, housing, public schools and voting rights. Throughout the 1960s, Dr. King continued to work for the rights of Black Americans, advocating change through nonviolent protest.

In 1964, Dr. King was awarded the Noble Peace Prize for his work in overcoming unfairness and discrimination through nonviolent means. The Nobel Prize is probably the most recognized achievement award in the world. Each year this distinguished prize is awarded to a person or group of persons who have done the most for world peace. Dr. King received a medal and a monetary award of $54,000. He believed the money and the award belonged to all Black Americans so he distributed the money to several Black organizations that were known to promote his views of nonviolent change. Dr. King was also chosen as "Man of the Year," by Time Magazine the same year.

On April 4, 1968, Dr. Martin Luther King, Jr. was tragically killed by a sniper outside a Memphis motel in Tennessee. The news of his death shocked the world. More than 100,000 people attended his funeral in Atlanta, Georgia.

Today his birthdate of January 15th is observed throughout the United States. It is a time for people everywhere to remember a great man and his great ideas of freedom and fairness for all people.

Write your own thoughts about Dr. Kings statement "...they will not be judged by the color of their skin but by the content of their character..."

_____

_____

_____

_____

_____

Dr. Martin Luther King, Jr.
"I Have a Dream..."

Dr. King's dream was to have all people treated with respect and judged only by their character not the color of their skin. Tell about a dream you have that will make our world a better place to live.

I have a dream that someday...

_____

_____

_____

_____

_____

This is what I will do to help make this dream a reality.

_____

_____

_____

_____

_____

Dr. Martin Luther King, Jr.

"I Have a Dream" Pledge

**I promise to work harder
at finding peaceful solutions
to problems at home
and at school.**

**I also promise to not judge
other people unfairly
and to help make
Dr. King's dream a reality.**

_____   _____
Signed   Date

"I Have a Dream" Pledge

Martin Luther King had a dream that all men and women, boys and girls, could live together in peace and harmony. He asked that we not judge one another by the color of our skin but rather the content of our character. He also encouraged all people to solve their problems peaceably.

Discuss Martin Luther King's dream with your students. Tell them that they can help to make Dr. King's dream a reality at school and at home. Ask them to make a pledge to not judge other students unfairly and to work harder at finding peaceful means to solving problems in the classroom and on the playground.

Award this badge to children who promise to work for peaceful solutions and brotherhood.

Ask older children to bring in newspaper and magazine articles about people in the world who are not free. Have them locate information about apartheid in South Africa and persecution in communist countries.

They might like to research people that have demonstrated great courage and have risked their lives for freedom and justice, such as Abraham Lincoln, Harriet Tubman, Mohandas Gandhi, Joan of Arc and Reverend Tutu.

Badge Pattern

January 15th
Martin Luther King Day
"I have a dream..."

Name

Martin Luther King Day Activities!

CIVIL RIGHTS VOCABULARY WORDS

Ask your students to define the following words that relate to Dr. King's life and work:

EQUALITY   PEACE
CIVIL RIGHTS   PREJUDICE
BOYCOTT   PROTEST
CHARACTER   DEMONSTRATION
JUSTICE   OPPORTUNITY

Instruct students to write a report about Dr. King using several of these words.

NOBEL PEACE PRIZE

Dr. Martin Luther King, Jr. was awarded the Nobel Peace Prize in 1964. Older children may like to research other recipients of this distinguished award. Assign a given year to each student and ask them to find out about the person or persons that received the award for that year. Instruct the students to write reports about the award winners and the reasons they were chosen. Assemble the reports in chronological order and display them on the class board with the title, "Peace For The World!"

I HAVE A DREAM.....

Read to your students a portion of the speech given by Dr. Martin Luther King in Washington, D.C. in 1963. Explain to them that when speaking of his "dream," Dr. King did not mean a dream such as the ones we have when we sleep, but rather a wish or hope. Ask children to take each letter in the word "DREAM" and write a sentence about a hope they have for themselves, their families or their community.

,HAPPY BIRTHDAY MARTIN!

Encourage your students to participate in singing "Happy Birthday, Martin Luther King" on his special day, January 15th. Students may like to write simple poems that can then be put to familiar tunes in tribute to Dr. King.

At the end of the day, let your students celebrate Dr. King's accomplishments by having a class party. Provide chocolate and vanilla cupcakes that can be frosted by your students and decorated with sugar sprinkles or red hots.

VIOLENCE OR NONVIOLENCE

Discuss with your students the various ways to solve problems or disagreements. Encourage them to look for ways to promote nonviolence and compromise when settling disputes. Here are a few examples of problems that can be discussed in the classroom. Encourage students to add their own scenarios for discussion.

You have a friend who dislikes people that have a different skin color. He often calls them names and says mean things about them. What do you do?

There is an older student that has threatened you and wants to fight you after school. What do you do?

Your school has a new rule that seems to be unfair to the students in your grade level. What do you do?

You are really angry at a student in your class because she teased you about your old tennis shoes. What do you do?

"Dream" Mobile

Each student can make his or her own "I HAVE A DREAM...MOBILE" using these simple patterns. Cut the mobile from white construction paper and assemble with yarn, as shown.

Read Martin Luther King's story to your class and ask the students to reflect on the "dream" that Dr. King had for our country. Ask each student to write his or her own "dream" for the community, country and world on the appropriate mobile pieces.

Tell them that their "dream" must be one that can succeed only if people care for one another and work together in harmony. Examples might include: world hunger, war, poverty, a clean environment, etc.

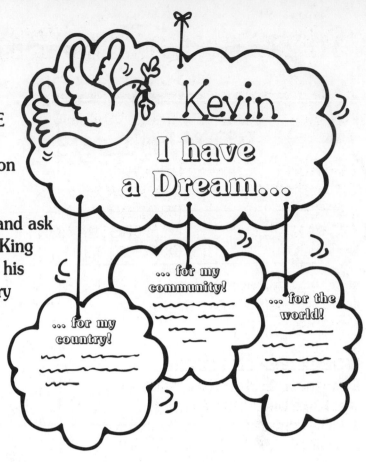

Name

"I have
a Dream . . ."

You can also make a
booklet cover with this
pattern.

TF0100 January Idea Book

My Report on the Life of Dr. Martin Luther King, Jr.

Martin Luther King was born

in _____

on _____ .

His father was a _____ .

In _____ , he married _____ .

Together they had _____ children.

Dr. King is famous for.... _____

_____

He gave his most famous speech in_____

in 1963. People call it his "_____" speech.

He was awarded the _____ _____ _____ in 1964.

I admire him because _____

_____

_____

_____

Dr. King was murdered in _____ when he was

only _____ years old.

Eskimos!

The Eskimo People!

For thousands of years, small groups of people have lived in the cold northern areas of Alaska, Canada, Greenland and Siberia. The Eskimos have been the only people successful in finding food, clothing and shelter in these frozen lands.

The "Inuit",, or Eskimos, of Alaska and Canada are the most well known. The word "Inuit" means "real people." The word "Eskimo" is an Indian word meaning "eaters of raw meat."

Winters are severely cold in these northern regions. The temperature often remains 25° below zero for weeks at a time. Yet the Eskimos are able to build homes and find food which allows them to live in this harsh climate.

Summer in the Arctic circle is much warmer than winter, but very short. When the snow melts, the "tundra" is exposed to allow some plants and grasses to grow.

Eskimos do not live in igloos made of snow, as most people think. Ice houses are built only as temporary shelters during winter hunting trips. The "igloo" is made from blocks of snow which are carefully cut and formed into a small round house with a hole in the top for a chimney.

Permanent homes are usually built of wood and whalebone and covered with seal skins and earth. Family members sleep on raised platforms in one large room. Seal oil is burned for warmth and light.

The clothing used in these harsh climates is very warm and protective. The Eskimo people must protect themselves from the severe cold with parkas, boots and mittens made from fur and animal hides. Snow goggles are used to protect their eyes from the glaring snow.

Finding food has always been a struggle for the Eskimos. At times, they patiently wait for hours in the cold to capture a walrus, seal or polar bear. Eskimos kill animals only for food or other useful products like oil, hides, and fur. In the summer, they catch fish, rabbits and even wild reindeer!

Eskimos use snowshoes to travel short distances on land. Long-distant travel is done with dog sleds. Huskies are the only animals that Eskimos have domesticated. The dogs are carefully trained to work as a team to pull the sleds long distances.

Two different types of boats are used to travel by water. The *kayak* is a one-man canoe which is extremely light and waterproof. It is made of driftwood and sealskin that fits tightly around the waist of the person inside. If the boat overturns, he or she will stay dry. The *umiak* is a large boat in which the entire family can travel. It is made of driftwood, whalebone and walrus skin.

Eskimos are generally warm and gentle people. Families usuallylive together in peaceful harmony while outsiders are made to feel welcome. Little has changed in their lives in modern times. They understand that each person depends on the others for his or her survival in the cold, harsh arctic climate.

Eskimo Word Find!

ACTIVITY 5

FIND THESE ESKIMO WORDS IN THE PUZZLE BELOW: ESKIMO, INUIT, IGLOO, SEAL, WALRUS, POLAR BEAR, PARKA, HUSKIES, KAYAK, UMIAK, ALASKA, CANADA, TUNDRA.

```
A C F T G B V C T U N D R A D C V R Y U J
P F G H Y T D F T G H N J L X C F G H B N
O K M J N I G L O O S D F A E F T G H J J
L D R F G H J K I L R F G S F P A R K A K
A F V G Y B H U J K I L O K C V B H N J A
R D V G B H N M J K L C F A G B C F T G Y
B E A X F T W A L R U S C F T G B H U J A
E C V B N M J K L O P M J N H B G V F R K
A D C G Y U I K L O P M B G C A N A D A T
R S C V G B H N J U M I A K P M N H J Y E
E S K I M O S E R C T V B H N J M K L G F
A E V G S S F T G H J H U S K I E S F T H
Q A C Z S E W D F D V B N M K L P O I Y T
A L H J S D F V B N I N U I T D R G B F D
```

Word Find!

Using six of the words in the puzzle, write a paragraph on what you have learned about the Eskimo people.

_____

_____

_____

_____

_____

_____

_____

Eskimo Crafts!

SCRIMSHAW MEDALLIONS

The Eskimo people have always enjoyed the fine art of carving. They use the ivory ffrom whales and walruses to make useful and decorative crafts. During the 18th century, the Eskimos taught carving and scrimshaw skills to many European sailors. These sailors made beautiful belt buckles and jewelry to take back home to their loved ones.

Making scrimshaw medallions in the classroom can be quite easy and a lot of fun!

Mix about 1 cup of plaster of Paris for every 2/3 cup of water. Quickly drop spoonfuls of the plaster onto sheets of wax paper. Use a nail or drinking straw to make a hole before it dries.

After it has dried overnight, let the children scratch designs in the plaster using a nail or paper clip. When the design is complete, rub colored chalk over the design and blow away the dust. A clear plastic spray can be applied, if you like. Thread a leather or yarn string through the hole and wear with pride!

ESKIMO SNOW GLASSES

The Inuit people, or Eskimos, made snow glasses that protected their eyes from the reflected glare of the snow. Your students can make snow glasses, too, with just a few simple materials.

Cut strips of poster board or laminated construction paper measuring about 3" x 16". Cut out as the pattern indicates.

Children can color or paint their own creative designs on the glasses.

Children will love wearing their "snow glasses" whether it be in the winter or the sunny summer.

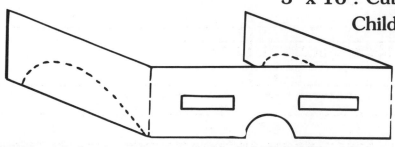

Cut out eye slots with an art knife.

My Eskimo Report

The Eskimo people live in these areas:

_____

_____

_____

The weather in these areas is...

_____

_____

Eskimo homes are _____

_____

_____

The Eskimo people wear _____

_____

_____

The word "Eskimo" means...

_____

_____

The word "Inuit" means...

_____

_____

The Eskimo people travel in different ways. Here's an example:

_____

_____

_____

Eskimos hunt for their food. Here is a list of what they hunt:

_____   _____

_____   _____

_____   _____

Here are my thoughts on the Eskimo way of life.

_____

_____

_____

Eskimo Story Characters

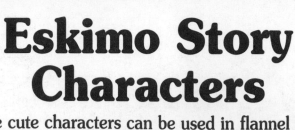

These cute characters can be used in flannel board stories about Eskimo life. Cut out and color each illustration. Glue a square of flannel to the back of the picture and apply to the board as you tell the story of the Inuit people.

Enlarged, these characters can be used in a bulletin board display. It's a great way to reinforce the concepts involving various Eskimo words and customs.

Eskimos wear fur jackets called "parkas."

Seals provide Eskimos with much of their food as well as skins for their clothing.

The meat and skin of the walrus is very valuable to the Eskimos. Their tusks provide the ivory for scrimshaw and carving.

The Eskimos are very warm and gentle people.

Common names for Eskimo children include Ootah, Nathlook, Inatuk, and Akoik.

"Mukluks" help keep their feet warm in the cold winters.

A "kayak" is a small one-person boat made of driftwood and seal skin. It is extremely light and waterproof.

"Igloos" are temporary homes made from blocks of snow. Eskimos build igloos when they are on long hunting trips.

Sleds pulled by "huskies" are used to travel great distances across the snow.

Eskimo

TF0100 January Idea Book

Totem Pole

For centuries, Eskimos have carved beautiful totem poles from tall cedar logs. They carve the poles as a way to preserve and celebrate their cultural heritage. The figures carved in each totem pole depict the animals and characters of ancient legends and tribal history.

Looking at the totem pole on this page, ask your students to write a legend using the figures depicted as inspiration. You will be intrigued by the variety of interpretations made by your individual students.

Have students color the totem pole with bright colors.

Arctic (and Antarctic) Animals!

Arctic and Antarctic Animals!

Your students will be fascinated to learn about the amazing animals living in the Arctic and Antarctic. Here are a few ideas to get you started:

ARCTIC AND ANTARCTICA
Remind students about the frigid weather associated with both areas. Tell them that the poles are covered with ice all year round.

At the South Pole, the ice covers a large land mass called Antarctica. It is the coldest place on earth. Even though scientists often visit the area to study it, no people live in Antarctica.

At the North Pole, there is no land, only huge sheets of floating ice. This area is called the Arctic. Eskimos are the only people that have been able to consistantly endure the harsh, cold winters. They travel across the ice to hunt seals and caribou.

Use the two maps contained in this chapter to help explain where these areas are located. Instruct students to find both the Arctic and Antarctic on a world globe.

ANIMAL LIFE
The animals of the Arctic include polar bears, whales, seals, the Arctic fox, the Arctic hare, caribou, the Arctic wolf and walrus.

The animals of Antarctica include seals, whales, several birds and many varieties of penguins.

Collect a number of animal resource books from the school library and ask your students to choose an Arctic or Antarctic animal to research. Have each child draw a picture of his or her animal. Pin the maps of both areas on the class board and display the research papers and the drawings around the maps. Stretch lengths of yarn from each paper to the animals' locations and habitats.

COLOR OF THE POLAR BEAR
The polar bear is white for a reason! Have your students speculate as to why the polar bear has white fur. Ask them to think of other animals that have colors that camouflage them in the wild.

Cut a number of bear patterns from white paper. Cut a few more from both black and brown paper. Now, at the front of the class, tape a large sheet of white paper to the board. During recess, paste or tape all of the bears to the white paper. When the students return to class, ask them to quickly take their seats and add up all of the bears they see on the white paper. They will be amazed at how many white bears they miss!

PENGUIN MATH
Most penguins average 30 feathers per square centimeter (or about 180 per square inch). Ask your students to estimate how many feathers a penguin might have. Observe the number of creative they can find the overall area of a penguin. (Of course, the size of an Emperor penguin will be different from that of an Adelie penguin).

Arctic and Antarctic Animals!

WALRUS FACTS

Did you know that the walrus is a large seal with tusks? His tusks can measure as long as 40 inches! Walruses have short, stiff whiskers that are very sensitive and help them to find food. They have very little hair on their bodies. A male walrus can grow as large as 3,500 pounds and over 12 feet in length. Walruses eat clams, starfish and sea urchins. They use their large tusks to defend themselves against polar bears and human hunters.

Have students measure 12 feet on the class floor. Instruct them to estimate what other object might weigh 3,000 pounds. (A small car would be one.) Show students that a walrus' tusks would measure longer than a yardstick.

SEAL FACTS

Seals are much smaller than walruses. They eat fish and other sea animals. They must swim under the ice for long periods of time in search for food and can hold their breath for almost an hour. Seals dig breathing holes in the ice to get a breath of air. Polar bears often hunt seals by waiting by a breathing hole for a seal to surface. Seals are the favorite food of killer whales, but their natural enemies also include sharks and man. Baby fur seals have been hunted for their skin for centuries.

Students may like to write to one of the organizations that are attempting to protect endangered sea animals, such as:

Greenpeace
1611 Connecticut Ave., N.W.
Washington, D.C. 20009

TYPES OF PENGUINS

Your students will enjoy learning about several types of penguins and their habitats. Begin by asking the children to list what they already know about penguins. Write the list on the class board. You are sure to get responses which include:

"They are all black and white."
"They live at the North Pole."
"They only fly when in danger."
"Eskimos hunt them."

You will soon learn that the students don't know as much as they think. Divide the class into groups and give each group a penguin to research.

Adelie Penguins are hyperactive smaller birds that live in the Antarctic.

Emperor Penguins are very regal and stand at over three and one-half feet tall.

Crested Penguins have fiery-red eyes and orange or yellow crests on their heads.

Yellow-Eyed Penguins have bright yellow eyes and a yellow crown. They generally live in South New Zealand.

Magellanic Penguins are most commonly seen in zoos and prefer warmer climates.

After each group has reported its findings, compare their facts to the statements on the board. Did they learn anything new?

Arctic and Antarctic Animals!

THE ANTARCTIC

Penguins are not the only animals living in the Antarctic. Seals, whales and other birds live there, also.

Ask your students to discover more about the mysterious area known as the Antarctica. Have them find out the answers to these questions:

Who discovered Antarctica?
Are there cities there?
How cold does it get? How warm?
How large is the area?
How much of the area is covered with ice and snow?

Students may also like to find out about ice shelves, glaciers, icecaps, etc.

HEMISPHERES

When studying penguins, one must remember that not all penguins love ice and snow. Some live in warmer climates. Penguins, however, are found only in the Southern Hemisphere.

Using a globe, show the students the line marking the equator. Point out how south of this line signifies the Southern Hhemisphere and north of it the Northern Hhemisphere. You may like to continue this exercise into east and west and latitudes and longitudes.

A clever way to teach these concepts is with navel oranges. Give each child a navel orange and a ball-point pen or fine tipped marker. Following your instructions, have them draw a line marking the equator of their orange. Have them each mark north and south, east and west. Latitude and longitude lines can also be drawn.

When everyone understands the concepts, let them peel their oranges and enjoy a refreshing treat!

EXPLORING THE POLES

Encourage your students to research the lives of the people that risked it all to reach both the South and North Poles. They may like to see the explorers' routes on the maps included in this chapter. Instruct them to find out about the following explorers:

Roald Amundsen, a Norwegian explorer, was the first person to reach the South Pole, in 1911.

In 1929, Naval Officer Richard E. Byrd was the first to fly over the South Pole. He later led expeditions for the United States government.

There were several explorers during the 1500-1800s that attempted to find a water route through the frozen northern seas. Find out about Martin Frobisher, Samuel Hearne, Sir John Franklin and Nils A.E. Nordenskjold.

In 1909, Navy Commander Robert E. Peary and his small crew were the first to reach the North Pole.

In 1958, the U.S. atomic submarine Nautilus traveled nearly 2,000 miles under the Arctic icecap.

In 1978, a Japanese explorer named Naomi Uemura became the first person to reach the North Pole alone by dog sled.

Walrus Puppet

Cut this walrus puppet pattern from colored construction paper.

Glue both pieces to a small paper lunch bag and color. Short sections of black string can be glued in place for whiskers.

Stand-Up Penguin

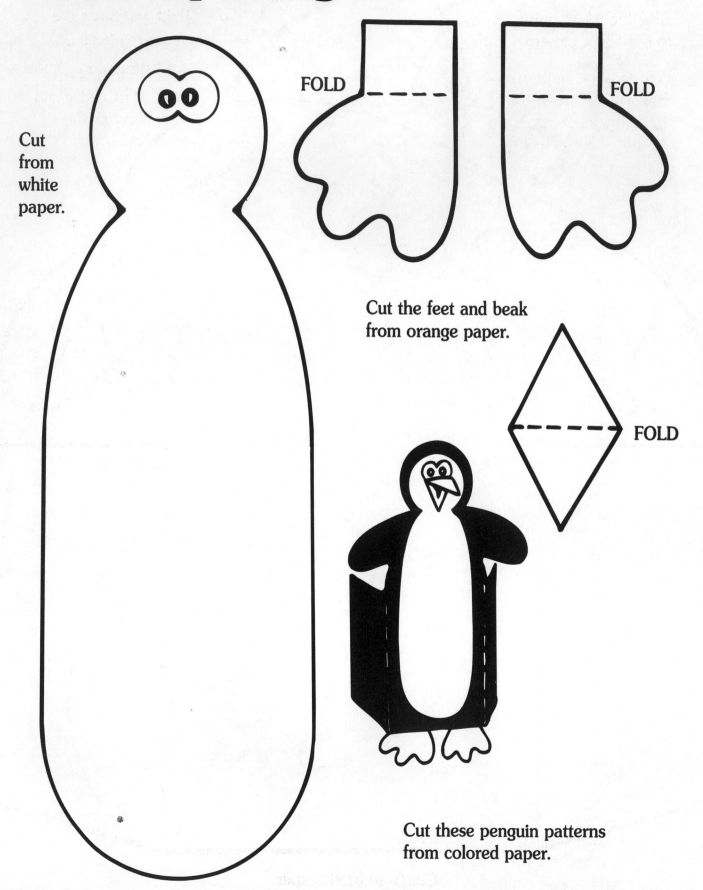

Cut
from
white
paper.

FOLD

FOLD

Cut the feet and beak
from orange paper.

FOLD

Cut these penguin patterns
from colored paper.

TF0100 January Idea Book

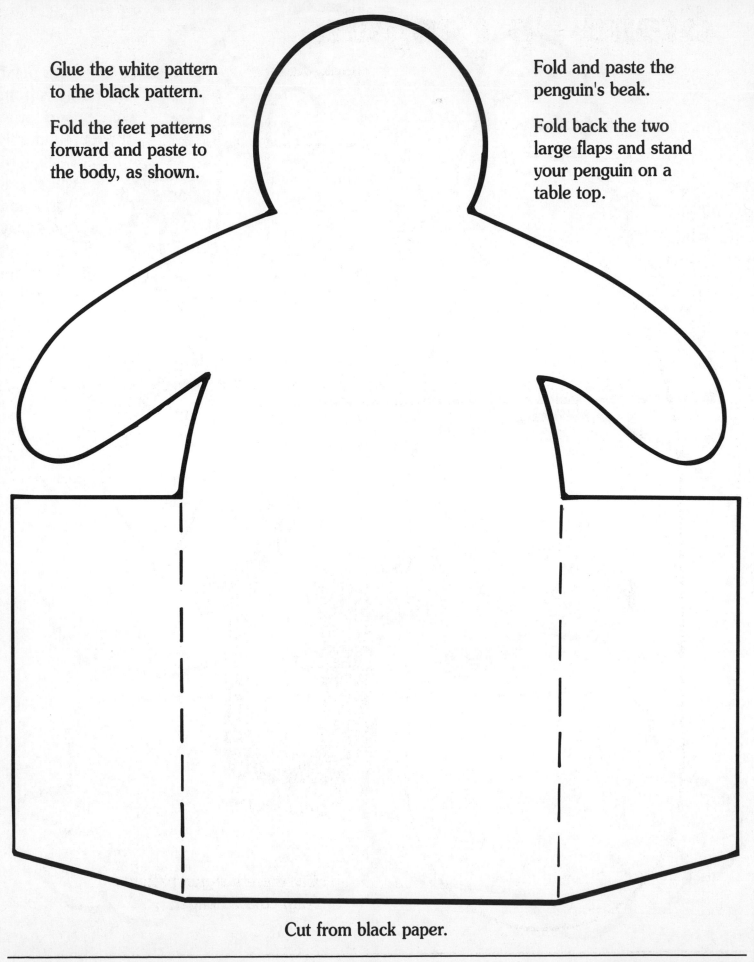

Glue the white pattern to the black pattern.

Fold the feet patterns forward and paste to the body, as shown.

Fold and paste the penguin's beak.

Fold back the two large flaps and stand your penguin on a table top.

Cut from black paper.

Cut these polar bear patterns from white paper. Paste them around a 9" x 12" sheet of white construction paper. Display a research paper on the construction paper.

**Polar
Bear
Page Topper**

TF0100 January Idea Book

Penguin Booklet

Name

FOLD

Map of Antarctica

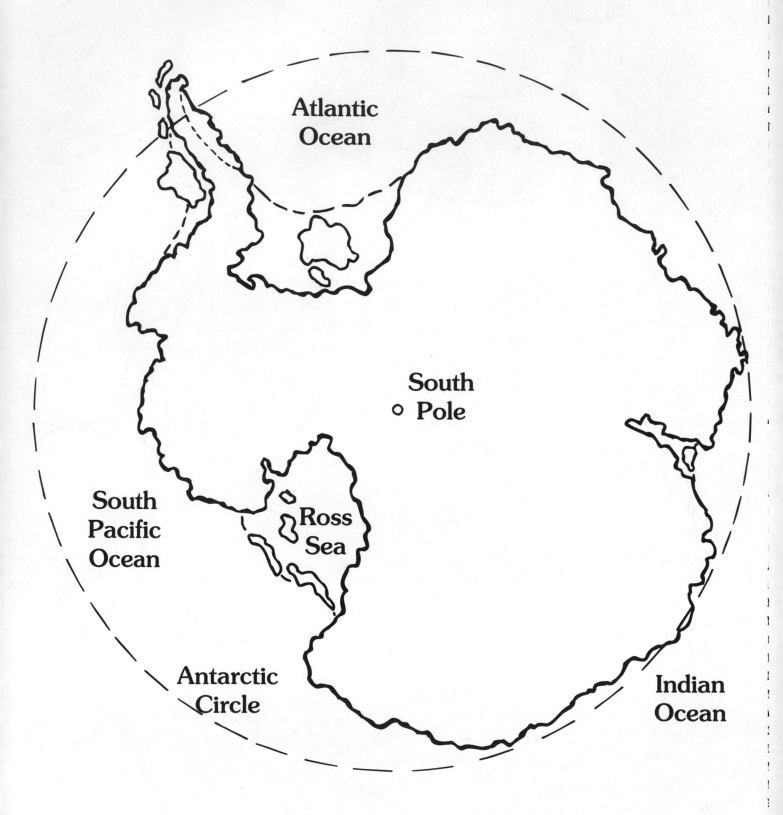

Atlantic Ocean

South Pole

South Pacific Ocean

Ross Sea

Antarctic Circle

Indian Ocean

Map
of the
Arctic

Alaska

Russia

Canada

Arctic Ocean
(frozen year-round)

North
Pole
○

Russia

Buffin
Bay

Greenland

Barents
Sea

Arctic
Circle

Norway

Iceland

TF0100 January Idea Book

Walrus Writing Page

Bulletin Boards and more!

Ring In the New Year!

A- Mike

B+ Ann

A Sally

A- Beth

A Lee

B+ Luis

A Suzy

B+ Maria

Bulletin Boards and More!

CLASSROOM TOTEM POLE

Make an impressive classroom totem pole by asking students to bring in assorted cardboard boxes. The boxes can be covered with construction paper and cut-paper faces glued in place. Assemble the totem pole with masking tape. Place it in a corner of the room for added stability.

What a fun way to end a unit on Eskimos!

FOOTSTEPS TO FOLLOW

Paper footsteps announcing values of famous leaders will help inspire youngsters to follow in their footsteps.

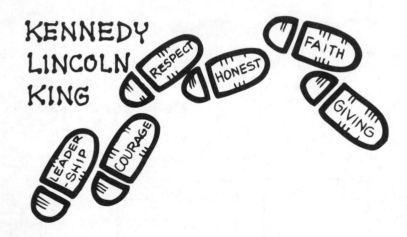

KENNEDY
LINCOLN
KING

RESPECT
HONEST
FAITH
GIVING
LEADER-SHIP
COURAGE

SIMPLE MONITOR DISPLAY

Cut colored paper plates in half. Write each student's name on one plate half and a classroom job on the remaining half. Match the two halves together and pin them to the class board. Change the classroom duties often, to give everyone a chance.

Calendar
Julie

Line Leader
Jimmy

Flag Salute
Robbie

Bulletin Boards and More!

RAINBOW RACES

Brighten up a winter classroom with a colorful rainbow bulletin board. Students cut their own snowflakes that compete to reach the pot of gold. Each snowflake moves ahead as library books are read or multiplication facts learned.

Next month, change the snowflakes to paper hearts and then to shamrocks in March.

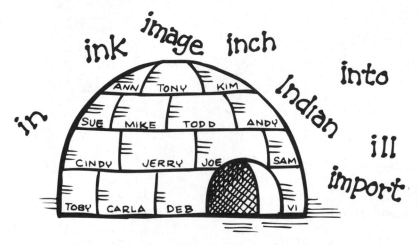

SHORT "I" IGLOO

Ask children to write short "i" words on strips of paper and display them on the class board around a giant paper igloo. As words are collected, write the students' names on the blocks of ice.

The same igloo can be used to display Eskimo reports or winter poems.

COMING SOON!

Look ahead to the new year by listing the highlights of the months to come.

Keep interest high by frequently changing the events.

Bulletin Boards and More!

WHAT A GREAT YEAR!

Enlarge a world globe on the class bulletin aboard. Display the year across the top of the board.

Students can collect articles from newspapers and magazines teling about events that have taken place during the year. Display the articles around the board.

FOR ALL SEASONS...

Prepare a large pattern for each month of the year that the children can trace onto colored paper. Children should choose the pattern that matches their birth month. Once the patterns are cut out, tell the children to write their birth date at the top. They should also include information about themselves such as the number of family members, favorite school subjects, favorite color and food. Display the seasonal patterns on the class board and instruct students to guess which personal description matches which student.

A CLASS FOR ALL SEASONS!

I HAVE A DREAM...

Ask each student to write a one-page report about Martin Luther King. Display the reports in construction paper folders spelling out his name.

Label the top of the board "I have a dream..." and your bulletin board is complete.

Snowman Mobile

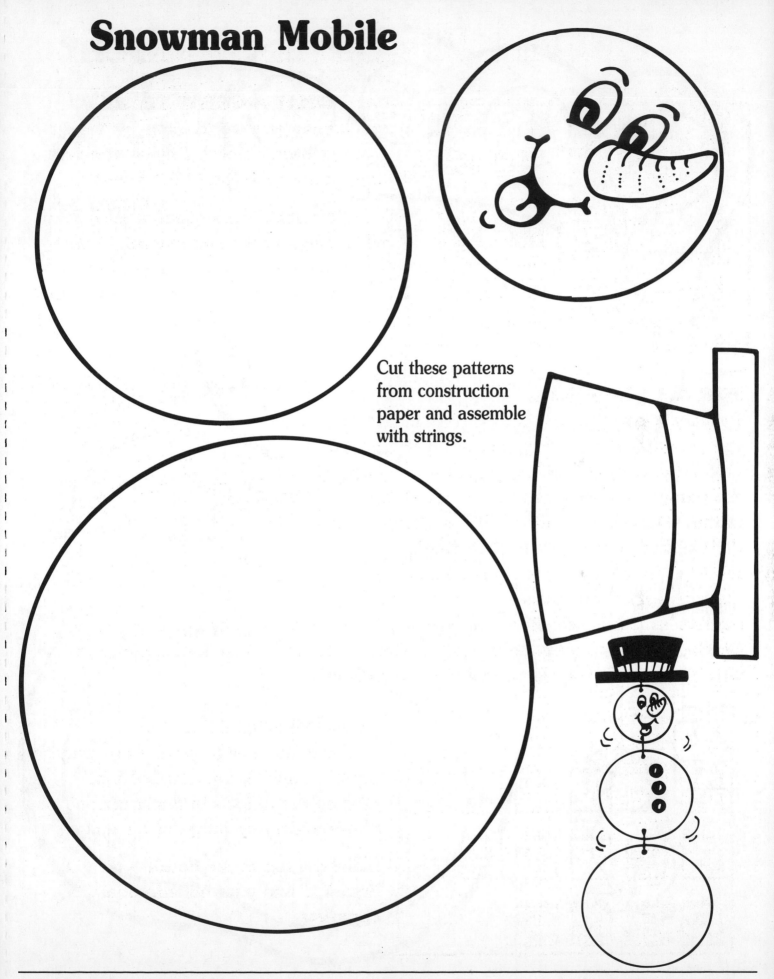

Cut these patterns
from construction
paper and assemble
with strings.

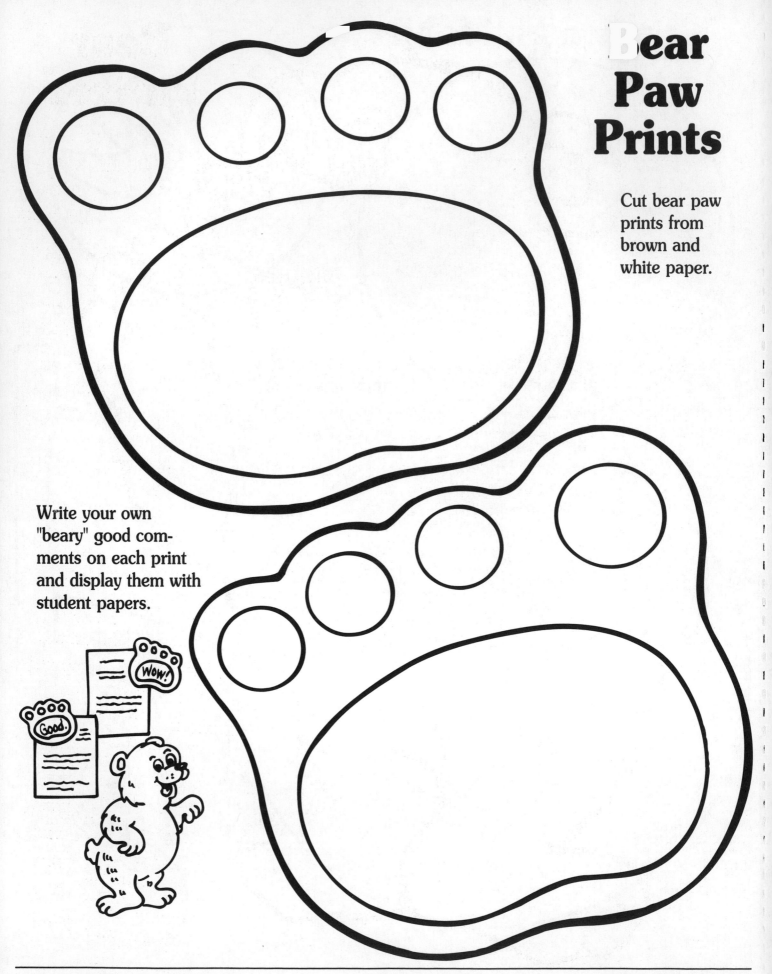

Bear Paw Prints

Cut bear paw prints from brown and white paper.

Write your own "beary" good comments on each print and display them with student papers.

Wow!

Good.

Bear Pattern

Dog Sled Team Patterns

Use these patterns in a variety of ways.

1. Give each student their own sled and driver. Let them collect dogs to race across the class bulletin board.

2. Enlarge the patterns and label the sled with your name and room number. Copy and cut one dog pattern for each student in the class. Label them with the students' names. Display the entire dog sled team down one wall to welcome new-comers to your class.

(Cut the patterns from heavy paper or enlarge them for bulletin board displays.)

3. Write math problems in the sled patterns and the answers on the dog patterns. Students match the dogs to the appropriate sled after solving the math problems.

Sleepy Time!

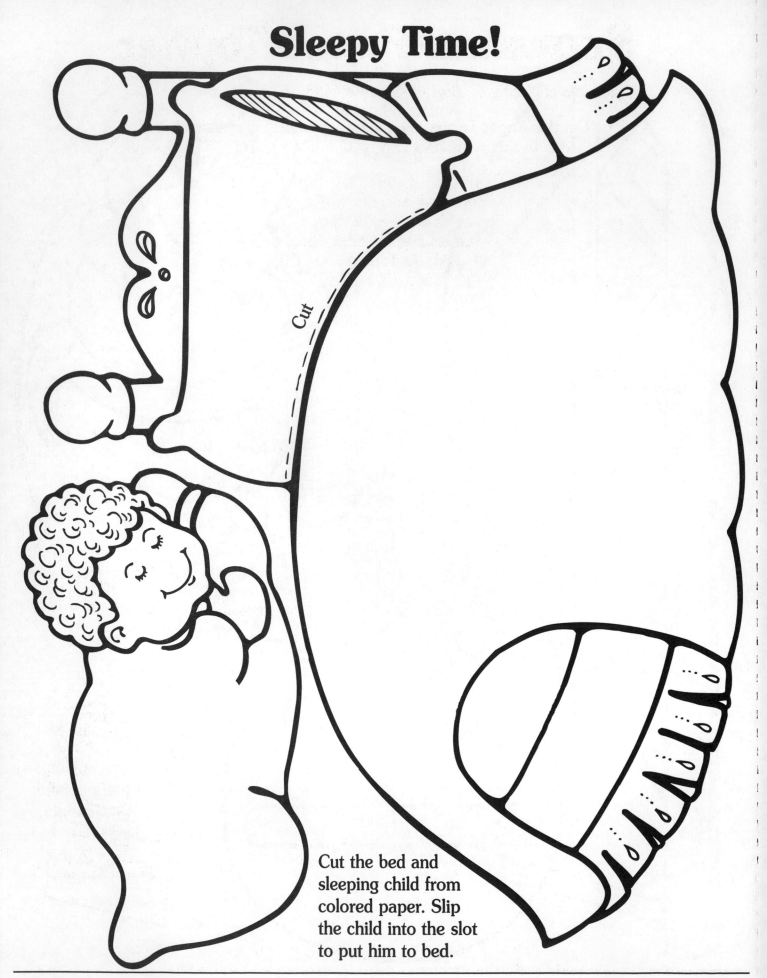

Cut the bed and
sleeping child from
colored paper. Slip
the child into the slot
to put him to bed.

Snowman Paper Topper

Here's a cute way to display students' work this winter!

Cut this Paper Topper from colored paper. Or, students can use crayons or markers to add the color.

Fold along the dotted lines, tape the back together and insert over the corner of a student's good work paper! Display the papers with the toppers on the class board.

Winter Patterns

Use those Winter Patterns to create mobiles, awards, nametags, calendar symbols or matching activities.

TF0100 January Idea Book

Chinese Lettering

138

140

142

Answer Key!

ACTIVITY 1

FIND THESE WINTER WORDS IN THE PUZZLE: SNOW, ICE, MITTENS, WINTER, FROST, COLD, JACKET, SLED, ICICLE, SNOWFLAKE, SKI, SNOWMAN.

```
C M D F G (S N O W M A N) D R T F G T Y H J U
M D E F R G T (S K I) B H Y N (F) D R V B N M F
I G H J D F G H G T H Y J R D T G H J K L
T D C V (W I N T E R) D C X Z O F T H J K L O
T D F G H J T H Y G H J K U S L E D D S A E
E M N B V C F T F C D R F C T S D A W E I K
N S D D F C G B H O J M K H V F T R D R C V
(S N O W F L A K E) L V C S W E S A X C Z E V
Z X C V B Y T G H D S V B N H Y U J K L T S
A S X C (J A C K E T) S D F V B H Y T G F E S
A S D F F G T R E C N K L M N S (I C I C L E)
A X D R T A C V (S N O W) B H Y T G F D E W S
```

ACTIVITY 2

FIND THE MONTHS OF THE YEAR IN THE PUZZLE BELOW: JANUARY, FEBRUARY, MARCH, APRIL, MAY, JUNE, JULY, AUGUST, SEPTEMBER, OCTOBER, NOVEMBER, DECEMBER.

```
A M S D F R E T G D C Q A S E D F R G B N M C D S (J
A X C (M A R C H) A C F V B G H N (J U N E) O U K I G A
(A) S S D E F R T G J S D E R T G B N H J U K I L I N
P S D (S E P T E M B E R) F G H Y J U K I O L G T U
R D F G T H Y J U D F R T G H Y N J U G C H Y U G A
I S W E D C V G T (D E C E M B E R) D R F T S W A W R
L S X C V B G F D S A W E R T G Y A D E O F R S E Y
X S A F R E T Y H G T R E D C F G T R A B R G H J S
G (J U L Y) A X (M Z S E R C V G Y H Y A R E F G V B N
X Z C V B G T A A (N O V E M B E R) K L E R A S E D F
A W S D F R C Y A S D C V F G D C V F G (A U G U S T)
A S X (F E B R U A R Y) C V B H J K L O P M N G F D S
```

© Teacher's Friend, a Scholastic Company   143   TF0100 January Idea Book

Answer Key!

ACTIVITY 3

BDREECEM	DECEMBER
TUUSGA	AUGUST
CMRAH	MARCH
TEROOCB	OCTOBER
RYUABRFE	FEBRUARY
NEUJ	JUNE
RLPAI	APRIL
VMEONREB	NOVEMBER
AMY	MAY
UYNJAAR	JANUARY
PMEESRBET	SEPTEMBER
LJYU	JULY

ACTIVITY 4

FIND THESE NEW YEAR WORDS IN THE PUZZLE BELOW: JANUARY, NEW YEAR, BELLS, CELEBRATE, MIDNIGHT, FATHER TIME, RESOLUTION, CONFETTI, BALLOONS, CUSTOM, FRIENDS.

```
G N M K L O P L K M J N H G A S W E R T X
A S W D V F R T F V G E N S E D F T G H Y U
F R I E N D S X D R T W U I C F T G B N B
Q E S D F R G T G H N E F R C U S T O M N
Q A A S E R C V B N H Y T F W S C V F R G D J
A A X O C V B C O N D V F W F R B D E R T Y Y
A X L C O N F E T T I D R S E E C V B N M I
Q U X C V B G F D E B A E F L A S D E R U
Q A Z T D F G H X E R T Y H C E L E B R A T E
A Z I X C V G T F R E D F G T S D V B N M U
A O F B N M J K F A T H E R T I M E X C T
W N S D B A L L O O N S C D R E T G H Y N
M I D N I G H T V D E R T F G R D S W E R
A S D E W Q X C V J A N U A R Y N H J K L
```

ACTIVITY 5

FIND THESE ESKIMO WORDS IN THE PUZZLE BELOW: ESKIMO, INUIT, IGLOO, SEAL, WALRUS, POLAR BEAR, PARKA, HUSKIES, KAYAK, UMIAK, ALASKA, CANADA, TUNDRA.

```
A C F T G B V C T U N D R A D C V R Y U J
P F G H Y T D F T G H N J L X C F G H B N
O K M J N I G L O O S D F A E F T G H J J
L D R F G H J K I L R F G S F P A R K A K
A F V G Y B H U J K I L O K C V B H N J A
R D V G B H N M J K L C F A G B C F T G Y Y
B E A X F T W A L R U S C F T G B H U J A
E C V B N M J K L O P M J N H B G V F R K
A D C G Y U I K L O P M B G C A N A D A T
R S C V G B H N J U M I A K P M N H J Y E
E S K I M O S E R C T V B H N J M K L G F
A E V G S S F T G H J H U S K I E S F T H
Q A C Z S E W D F D V B N M K L P O I Y T
A L H J S D F D V B N I N U I T D R G B F D
```

Word Find!